hamlyn
QuickCook

hamlyn

QuickCook

Healthy
Feasts

Recipes by Joy Skipper

Every dish, three ways – you choose!
30 minutes | 20 minutes | 10 minutes

An Hachette UK Company
www.hachette.co.uk

First published in Great Britain in 2013 by Hamlyn,
a division of Octopus Publishing Group Ltd
Endeavour House, 189 Shaftesbury Avenue
London WC2H 8JY
www.octopusbooks.co.uk

ISBN 978-0-600-62525-4

A CIP catalogue record for this book is available from the British Library

Printed and bound in China

10 9 8 7 6 5 4 3 2 1

Both metric and imperial measurements are given for the recipes. Use one set of
measures only, not a mixture of both.

Standard level spoon measurements are used in all recipes
1 tablespoon = 15 ml
1 teaspoon = 5 ml

Ovens should be preheated to the specified temperature. If using a fan-assisted oven,
follow the manufacturer's instructions for adjusting the time and temperature. Grills
should also be preheated.

This book includes dishes made with nuts and nut derivatives. It is advisable for those with
known allergic reactions to nuts and nut derivatives and those who may be potentially
vulnerable to these allergies, such as pregnant and nursing mothers, invalids, the elderly,
babies and children, to avoid dishes made with nuts and nut oils.

It is also prudent to check the labels of pre-prepared ingredients for the possible inclusion
of nut derivatives.

The Department of Health advises that eggs should not be consumed raw. This book
contains some dishes made with raw or lightly cooked eggs. It is prudent for more
vulnerable people such as pregnant and nursing mothers, invalids, the elderly, babies and
young children to avoid uncooked or lightly cooked dishes made with eggs.

Contents

Introduction

30 20 10 – Quick, Quicker, Quickest

This book offers a new and flexible approach to meal-planning for busy cooks, letting you choose the recipe option that best fits the time you have available. Inside you will find 360 dishes that will inspire and motivate you to get cooking every day of the year. All the recipes take a maximum of 30 minutes to cook. Some take as little as 20 minutes and, amazingly, many take only 10 minutes. With a bit of preparation, you can easily try out one new recipe from this book each night and slowly you will be able to build a wide and exciting portfolio of recipes to suit your needs.

How Does it Work?

Every recipe in the QuickCook series can be cooked one of three ways – a 30-minute version, a 20-minute version or a super-quick and easy 10-minute version. At the beginning of each chapter you'll find recipes listed by time. Choose a dish based on how much time you have and turn to that page.

You'll find the main recipe in the middle of the page accompanied by a beautiful photograph, as well as two time-variation recipes below.

If you enjoy your chosen dish, why not go back and cook the other time-variation options at a later date? So if you liked the 30-minute Horseradish Beef with Quinoa, but only have 10 minutes to spare this time around, you'll find a way to cook it using cheat ingredients or clever shortcuts.

If you love the ingredients and flavours of the 10-minute Salmon and Grapefruit Salad, why not try something more substantial, like the 20-minute Breaded Salmon with Grapefruit, or be inspired to make a more elaborate version, like the Salmon with Grapefruit Dressing and Roasted Vegetables? Alternatively, browse through all 360 delicious recipes, find something that catches your eye – then cook the version that fits your time frame.

Or, for easy inspiration, turn to the gallery on pages 12–19 to get an instant overview by themes, such as Mood Boosters or Super Foods.

QuickCook online

To make life even easier, you can use the special code on each recipe page to email yourself a recipe card for printing, or email a text-only shopping list to your phone. Go to www.hamlynquickcook.com and enter the recipe code at the bottom of each page.

HEA-SNAC-NIF

QuickCook Healthy Feasts

For the past few years, people have started to realize that the foods we eat can have a real effect on our health and how we function on a daily basis. Despite this, the number of people suffering from diabetes and cardiovascular disease is on the increase. Obesity is also a growing problem, particularly in the Western world.

The information about what we should and shouldn't eat seems to change on a regular basis, which can be confusing. However, eating a balanced, healthy diet is not difficult, and should be something you enjoy. The recipes provided in this book will help you to eat a variety of great nutritious foods, with minimum effort required to prepare and cook them.

A Healthy Diet

So what is the best way to ensure your diet is healthy and nutrient rich? The easiest way is to cook meals from scratch – it is not as difficult or time-consuming as you may think, and you can start by trying some of the recipes in this book.

Planning your weekly menu can also help you to eat a healthy, balanced diet. Meals for the week should include good-quality protein (fish, eggs, poultry, lentils and beans, and meat) and filling, but nutritious carbohydrates. Choose recipes that are made with unrefined foods (such as sweet potatoes, wholemeal pasta, brown rice and quinoa), essential fats (oily fish, such as salmon, sardines and mackerel), nuts (such as walnuts) and seeds (such as pumpkin, sesame and sunflower), and eat a variety of fresh fruit and vegetables to ensure your intake of vitamins and minerals is sufficient. Fruit and vegetables also provide daily fibre – very important for detoxifying unwanted toxins from the body. Drink plenty of water to help the fibre pass through the body.

Dairy products, such as cheese and yogurt, are important sources of calcium and vitamins, but some, in the case of butter and cream, have a high fat content, so should be eaten in smaller amounts. Some people find they are intolerant to dairy products, but these days there are lots of alternatives, such as soya, almond and rice milks, and dairy-free yogurts and cheeses.

The Mediterranean Diet

A research paper published in 2008 showed that following a strict Mediterranean diet reduces the risk of dying from cancer and cardiovascular disease, and the risk of developing Parkinson's and Alzheimer's disease. The diet is based on fresh produce and cooking great ingredients from scratch. It includes a high intake of olive oil, legumes, unrefined cereals, fruits and vegetables, a moderate intake of dairy products (mostly as yogurt and cheese) and a low consumption of meat.

The Role of Fat

We have never been more obsessed with dieting, eating low-fat foods and even trying to cut fat out of our diets completely. This is not a healthy way to eat. It is best to eat food in its most natural state – milk does not come out of a cow semi-skimmed! The fat you consume does not make you overweight (unless you are eating the wrong kind in huge amounts, of course); what does is eating too much sugar and not burning it off, causing it to turn to fat in the body. Research has shown that low-fat diets can lead to cravings, binge eating, risk of fat-soluble vitamin deficiency, depression, problems with blood-sugar regulation and skin problems.

Fat is one of the things that makes food tasty, and there is plenty of scientific evidence to show that we need it in our diets, but the important factor is the type of fat. Fats can be divided into two main types – saturated and unsaturated. Saturated fat is solid at room temperature and usually comes from animal sources. This fat is associated with an increased risk of heart disease. Unsaturated fats include the omega fats that are essential in the diet. We need healthy fat in our diet:

- For energy
- For body and organ insulation
- To keep toxins out of circulation
- For steroid hormone production
- To provide and circulate fat-soluble vitamins (vitamins A, D, E and K)
- For cell membrane structure, keeping cells supple
- To help fight against inflammation.

Healthy fats are found in oily fish, avocados, nuts and seeds.

Choosing Healthy Ingredients

Buy fresh, local produce that is in season – not only for its nutritional value (it is likely to have been picked more recently if it has not had to travel), but also for the flavour. Eating foods out of season usually means the product has been grown in and travelled from another country, and therefore has started to lose some of its nutrients and flavour.

Spend time at your local fishmonger's and butcher's shops, letting them know that you care about where your produce comes from, that it is sustainable and that you are willing to experiment with new foods. Take their advice about seasonal produce and hopefully you will learn how to cook new cuts of meats or fish that you previously would not have bought.

Try cooking with ingredients that have added health benefits (you will find recipes that use these in the book).

Coconut Oil: This is used widely in Indian cookery and is known to be antimicrobial, antifungal and antibacterial as well as an antioxidant, mainly due to the presence of lauric acid. It can be used as a substitute for butter or olive oil as it is not broken down into trans fats when heated.

Agave Syrup: Natural agave has been harvested in Mexico for hundreds of years. Ranking fairly low on the glycaemic index, a small amount provides more sweetness than sugar, so a little goes a long way. It is great stirred into cooked fruit or yogurt, but can also be used in cooking.

Avocados: These green-skinned, creamy fruits provide nearly 20 essential nutrients, including potassium, Vitamin E, fibre, B vitamins and folic acid, as well as unsaturated fats.

Oily Fish: Including mackerel, salmon, trout and sardines, this type of fish is rich in Omega 3 essential fats, which are required by the body for almost every function, from producing hormones to reducing inflammation. Omega 3 is also vital for a healthy, effective brain.

Rapeseed Oil: Unlike other vegetable oils, cold-pressed rapeseed oil contains Omega 3, 6 and 9 essential fats. While Omega 6 can be found in many food sources, it is harder to include Omega 3 in our diet, so the high ratio of Omega 3 to Omega 6 in rapeseed oil helps to redress this issue.

Nuts and Seeds: A healthy component of any diet, these are rich in minerals and essential fats.

If you buy ready-made foods, be sure to read the ingredient labels so you know what the food contains – aim for the least amount of preservatives and chemicals as possible. Learn what the different E numbers are (some of them are not harmful) and how they may affect you.

Food Preparation and Cooking

The way food is cooked affects how nutritious your diet is. Careful food preparation and cooking can help to retain certain nutrients. Follow the following guidelines for best results:

- Avoid peeling and chopping fruit and vegetables until the last minute before cooking, as exposed surfaces oxidize and lose vitamin C – you can see this when apples turn brown.
- Don't leave vegetables sitting in water as this causes them to leach vitamins.
- Cook for the minimum amount of time in the gentlest way possible – steaming is best.
- If you want to cook a stir-fry, you could add a little liquid such as water, stock or soy sauce, then cover and steam-fry instead, for a slightly healthy option.

How and When to Eat

Eating when you are in a relaxed state helps the body to absorb nutrients from the food, so eating 'on the go' or while you are doing something else is not good for your health. Take the time to relax and focus on what you are cooking and eating. Chewing food thoroughly helps it to be broken down in the body more efficiently and allows the nutrients to be absorbed more readily.

To help maintain energy levels throughout the day and prevent the body going into stress through hunger, aim to eat regularly, possibly every few hours, to keep your blood sugar in balance. Three meals a day and a couple of snacks is ideal. Breakfast should never be missed, and the old saying: 'Breakfast like a king, lunch like a prince and supper like a pauper' is a good one – aim to eat your main meal in the middle of the day.

Mood Boosters

Healthy, mood-enhancing feasts that are guaranteed to lift your spirits.

Nutty Granola 28

Smoked Mackerel and
Horseradish Pâté 32

Warm Smoked Duck and
Asparagus Salad 54

Spicy Chicken with Cucumber
and Radish Salad 114

Coronation Chicken with
Avocado Salad 126

Chicken Liver Salad with
Mustard Dressing 130

Grilled Lemon and Mustard
Sardines 154

Salmon and Grapefruit
Salad 160

Prawn and Goats' Cheese
Salad 176

Lemon and Raisin Scones 236

Cocoa, Orange and Pecan
Flapjack 242

Oaty Raspberry Dessert 278

Super Foods

Packed with nutrients, vitamins, and antioxidents, these dishes taste super too!

Broccoli and Black-Eyed Bean Soup 38

Smoked Haddock and Kale Soup 40

Avocado, Pepper and Olive Salad 50

Smoked Mackerel Superfood Salad 56

Beetroot and Goats' Cheese Salad 58

Calves' Liver with Caramelized Onions 124

Prawn and Spinach Curry 152

Grilled Salmon with Avocado Salsa 172

Asparagus and Pea Quinoa Risotto 202

Cheese and Spinach Quesadillas 214

Oat, Banana and Ginger Muffins 248

Wholemeal Blueberry Pancakes with Lemon Curd Yogurt 270

Weekend Treats

Fancy something special for the weekend? Look no further!

Breakfast Smoothies 26

Guacamole 34

Mini Smoked Trout Quiches 60

Rosemary Oatcakes 62

Griddled Courgette Bruschetta 72

Chicken Dippers with Homemade Hummus 90

Roast Pork Loin with Creamy Cabbage and Leeks 120

Smoked Haddock Welsh Rarebit 164

Mushroom, Tomato and Herb Pancakes 208

Pea and Mint Pancakes 210

Sesame Cookies 252

Wholemeal Raspberry Coconut Muffins 262

Good for Getting 5-A-Day

Kick-start your nutritious, balanced diet with these healthy feasts.

Hummus with Carrot and Celery Sticks 36

Salmon and Chickpea Salad 52

Pork, Apple and Ginger Stir-Fry 102

Chicken and Vegetable Stir-Fry 118

Cod Loin with Roasted Tomato Ratatouille 148

Smoked Mackerel and Spring Vegetable Tabbouleh 168

Butternut, Broccoli and Mushroom au Gratin 188

Simple Baked Leeks and Sweet Potatoes 222

Cheesy Spinach-Stuffed Mushrooms 226

Crunchy Pesto Broccoli with Poached Eggs 230

Berry and Mint Compote 254

Caramelized Autumn Fruits 274

Spicy Meals

These tasty, nutrient-rich dishes will leave you feeling hot hot hot!

Spiced Tuna Open Sandwiches 74

Spicy Barbecue Beans on Toast 76

Harissa Beef Fajitas 108

Ginger Chicken Soup 110

Salmon and Rice Bhajis 140

Keralan Fish Curry 162

Red Pepper and Coconut Curry 186

Moroccan Vegetable Stew 190

Butter Bean and Mushroom Tagine 198

Falafel with Spicy Sauce 228

Sweet Semolina with Cardamom Poached Apricots 244

Gingered Sesame Fruit Kebabs 268

Taste of the Med

Impart some healthy, Mediterranean magic into your food!

Gazpacho 44

Mediterranean Beans 68

Pancetta and Cannellini Bean Bruschetta 80

Chicken and Tarragon Risotto 100

Bacon and Leek Tortilla 112

Moules Marinières 136

Salmon Ceviche 144

Baked Sole with Fennel Pesto 150

Broad Bean and Feta Tagliatelle 192

Greek Pitta Pockets 204

Roasted Honey Peaches 250

Strawberry and Almond Desserts 258

Light Summer Dishes

These fresh summer dishes will put a spring in your step!

Melon, Mint and Strawberry Smoothies 24

Warm Lentil, Tomato and Haloumi Salad 46

Peach, Feta and Watercress Salad 48

Chorizo and Olive Tapenade Toasts 70

Prawn and Courgette Spring Rolls 84

Lamb Cutlets with Pea and Rosemary Mash 104

Chicken with Orange and Olives 106

Nectarine-Glazed Chicken Kebabs 122

King Prawn Caesar Salad 166

Roasted Peppers 196

Berry Eton Mess 240

Tropical Fruit Salsa 260

Light Winter Dishes

Hearty yet healthy food to warm you up on a cold winter's day.

Roasted Butternut, Sage and Cashew Soup 42

Chicken and Apricot Stew 96

Beef and Lentil Chilli 98

Fish Pie 174

Chunky Cod, Red Mullet and Prawn Stew 178

Cauliflower Cheese 194

Lentil, Mustard and Chickpea Soup 216

Mushroom and Tofu Stew 224

Oat-Topped Pear and Ginger Pudding 238

Blackberry Brûlées 246

Spicy Fruit Bread Puddings 256

Winter Fruits with Orange Ricotta 264

QuickCook

Snacks and Light Suppers

Recipes listed by cooking time

30

20

Melon, Mint and Strawberry Smoothies

Serves 4

1 small watermelon, peeled, deseeded and chopped
14–16 strawberries, hulled
12 mint leaves
small handful of ice

- Place all the ingredients in a blender and blend until smooth.
- Pour into 4 glasses and serve immediately.

20 Minty Melon and Strawberry Salad

Put 50 g (2 oz) caster sugar, 200 ml (7 fl oz) water and a 5-cm (2-inch) piece of fresh root ginger in a small saucepan and bring to the boil. Simmer for 5 minutes, then leave to cool slightly before removing the ginger. Divide ¼ peeled, deseeded and cubed watermelon, 16 hulled and halved strawberries and 12 mint leaves between 4 bowls. Pour over the ginger syrup and serve sprinkled with 2 tablespoons toasted flaked almonds.

30 Melon, Mint and Strawberry Soup

Place 1 small peeled, deseeded and chopped cantaloupe melon in a blender and blend until smooth. Pour into a jug, cover and chill for 20 minutes. Using a clean blender, repeat with 1 small peeled, deseeded and chopped honeydew melon and then 150 g (5 oz) hulled and chopped strawberries. When ready to serve, pour a ladle of each fruit purée into a bowl and make a pattern by dragging a knife through each one. Serve sprinkled with 2 tablespoons hulled and chopped strawberries and 2 teaspoons chopped mint.

Breakfast Smoothies

Serves 2–3

1 tablespoon pomegranate juice
1 small banana, chopped
300 ml (½ pint) soya milk
1 tablespoon almonds
1 tablespoon rolled oats
½ teaspoon honey
½ tablespoon ground linseeds
2 tablespoons natural yogurt

- Place all the ingredients in a blender and blend until smooth and creamy.

- Pour into 2 glasses and serve immediately.

2 Breakfast Muesli

Mix together 2 tablespoons rolled oats, 2 teaspoons ground linseeds, 1 tablespoon flaked almonds, 1 tablespoon goji berries and 2 peeled, cored and grated apples in a large bowl. Pour in 600 ml (1 pint) soya milk and leave to stand for 15 minutes. To serve, spoon into 2 bowls and top each one with 2 tablespoons natural yogurt, 1 small chopped banana and 1 teaspoon honey.

3 Breakfast Muffins

Mix together 125 g (4 oz) sifted wholemeal flour, 100 g (3½ oz) sifted plain flour, 2 teaspoons baking powder, 25 g (1 oz) rolled oats, 100 g (3½ oz) dark muscovado sugar, 50 g (2 oz) sultanas and 50 g (2 oz) flaked almonds in a large bowl. Beat together 100 g (3½ oz) melted coconut oil, 2 lightly beaten eggs and 2 tablespoons soya milk in a jug, then pour into the dry ingredients, add 4 mashed bananas and mix together until just combined – do not over-mix. Divide the mixture between 8 paper muffin cases arranged in a muffin tin and bake in a preheated oven, 190°C (375°F), Gas Mark 5, for 20 minutes or until golden. Transfer to a wire rack to cool.

3 ⦿ Nutty Granola

Serves 8–10

100 g (3½ oz) honey
150 g (5 oz) rolled oats
25 g (1 oz) flaked almonds
25 g (1 oz) sunflower seeds
25 g (1 oz) golden raisins
25 g (1 oz) dried cranberries
10 g (⅓ oz) chopped hazelnuts
1 teaspoon sesame seeds

To serve

natural yogurt
fresh fruit

- Melt the honey in a large saucepan over a low heat for 1–2 minutes. Add the remaining ingredients and mix together thoroughly.

- Spread the mixture out on a baking sheet and bake in a preheated oven, 180°C (350°F), Gas Mark 4, for 10–12 minutes until starting to turn golden. Stir the granola, turning it over a little, then return to the oven for a further 4–5 minutes.

- Pour on to a cool tray or into a large bowl and leave to cool. Store in an airtight container.

- Serve with natural yogurt and fresh fruit.

---

1 ⦿ Homemade Nutty Muesli

Mix together 200 g (7 oz) rolled oats, 25 g (1 oz) flaked almonds, 50 g (2 oz) sultanas, 50 g (2 oz) chopped ready-to-eat dried apricots, 2 tablespoons desiccated coconut, 25 g (1 oz) chopped walnuts, 1 tablespoon chopped hazelnuts and 2 teaspoons sesame seeds in a large bowl. Store in an airtight container. Serve with milk and fresh fruit.

2 ⦿ Nutty Muesli Muffins

Mix together 50 g (2 oz) self-raising flour, 75 g (3 oz) wholemeal plain flour, 2 teaspoons baking powder, 50 g (2 oz) ready-made nutty muesli and 75 g (3 oz) dark muscovado sugar in a large bowl. Beat together 100 ml (3½ fl oz) sunflower oil, 150 ml (¼ pint) soya milk and 1 egg in a jug, then pour into the dry ingredients and mix together until just combined – do not over-mix. Spoon into 10 paper muffin cases arranged in a muffin tin and bake in a preheated oven, 200°C (400°F), Gas Mark 6, for 15 minutes until well risen and golden.

 Smashed Bean and Sardine Dip

Serves 4

400 g (13 oz) can cannellini beans, rinsed and drained
400 g (13 oz) can chickpeas, rinsed and drained
2 garlic cloves, crushed
juice of 1 lime
1 teaspoon ground cumin
75 g (3 oz) canned sardines, drained
100 ml (3½ fl oz) thick natural yogurt
1 tablespoon chopped coriander
1 tablespoon olive oil
salt and pepper
vegetable crudités, to serve

• Place the beans and chickpeas, reserving 1 tablespoon of each, in a food processor. Add the garlic, lime juice, cumin, sardines and yogurt and process until smooth.

• Stir in the reserved beans and chickpeas with the coriander and season to taste. Transfer to a bowl and pour over the oil.

• Serve the dip with vegetable crudités.

---

2 Bean and Sardine Salad

Steam 200 g (7 oz) trimmed French beans until just tender. Drain and refresh under cold water, then drain again. Rinse and drain a 400 g (13 oz) can cannellini beans and a 400 g (13 oz) can kidney beans, then place in a bowl with the French beans, 200 g (7 oz) drained canned sardines, halved, 2 sliced celery sticks, 1 diced red onion, 1 diced apple and 2 tablespoons chopped parsley. Whisk together 1 tablespoon cider vinegar, 3 tablespoons olive oil, 1 teaspoon caster sugar and ½ teaspoon Dijon mustard, then toss into the salad. Serve sprinkled with 50 g (2 oz) toasted walnuts.

3 Sardine Bean Burgers

Lightly crush 2 rinsed and drained 400 g (13 oz) cans kidney beans with 125 g (4 oz) drained canned sardines in a large bowl. Mix in 75 g (3 oz) wholemeal breadcrumbs, 2 teaspoons chilli powder, 2 crushed garlic cloves, 1 tablespoon chopped coriander, 1 egg and 200 g (7 oz) chopped tomatoes and season. Divide the mixture into 4 and, using wet hands, shape into burgers. Cover and chill for 10 minutes. Meanwhile, to make a salsa mix together 2 cored, deseeded and diced red peppers, 2 peeled, stoned and diced avocados, 3 diced tomatoes, 1 tablespoon olive oil, the juice of ½ lime, 4 sliced spring onions and 1 tablespoon chopped coriander in a bowl. Cook the burgers under a preheated medium grill for 5–6 minutes on each side until golden. Toast 4 halved burger buns and spoon the salsa over the bases. Top each one with a burger and a dollop of soured cream, if liked. Replace the lids and serve.

Smoked Mackerel and Horseradish Pâté

Serves 4

500 g (1½ lb) smoked mackerel
  fillets
2 tablespoons natural yogurt
2 teaspoons creamed horseradish
juice of ½ lemon
pepper
oatcakes, toast or crudités,
  to serve

- Skin and flake the mackerel into a bowl. Add the remaining ingredients and mix well.

- Serve with oatcakes, toast or with crudités.

---

2 Smoked Mackerel with Horseradish

Mash Cook 750 g (1 lb 10 oz) peeled and chopped potatoes in a saucepan of boiling water for 12–15 minutes until tender. Meanwhile, cook 4 smoked mackerel fillets, about 120 g (4 oz) each, under a preheated medium grill for 2–3 minutes on each side until heated through. Place a large handful of basil leaves, 2 tablespoons toasted pine nuts, 1 garlic clove, 1 tablespoon grated Parmesan cheese and 3–4 tablespoons olive oil in a food processor or blender and blitz to form a pesto sauce. Drain the potatoes, then mash in the pan with 25 g (1 oz) butter, 1 tablespoon natural yogurt and 1 tablespoon creamed horseradish. Serve with the mackerel, drizzled with the pesto.

3 Warm Mackerel, Horseradish and

Potato Salad Cook 200 g (7 oz) new potatoes in a saucepan of boiling water for 15–20 minutes or until tender. Drain, then roughly chop and place in a large bowl with 2 peeled, cored and sliced apples, 1 tablespoon creamed horseradish and 2 tablespoons soured cream. Season to taste. Toss together 75 g (3 oz) salad leaves, 3 tablespoons olive oil, 1 tablespoon lemon juice, 1 teaspoon Dijon mustard and 1 teaspoon honey in a bowl. Grill 4 fresh mackerel fillets under a preheated hot grill for 2–3 minutes on each side. Divide the salad leaves between 4 plates, then top with the potato salad and mackerel. Serve with lemon wedges.

 Guacamole

Serves 4

2 ripe avocados, peeled, stoned
  and chopped
juice of 1 lime
6 cherry tomatoes, diced
1 tablespoon chopped coriander
1–2 garlic cloves, crushed
oatcakes or vegetable crudités,
  to serve

- Put the avocados and lime juice in a bowl and mash together to prevent discoloration, then stir in the remaining ingredients.

- Serve immediately with oatcakes or vegetable crudités.

20 Prawn and Avocado Salad

Soak 200 g (7 oz) vermicelli rice noodles in boiling water until just tender. Drain, refresh under cold running water and drain again, then place in a bowl with 200 g (7 oz) cooked peeled king prawns, 2 peeled, stoned and sliced avocados, ½ thinly sliced cucumber and 4 sliced spring onions. Next whisk together 100 ml (3½ fl oz) coconut milk, the juice of 1 lime and a 2-cm (1-inch) piece of fresh root ginger, peeled and grated, in a bowl. Pour over the salad and gently toss together to serve.

30 Smoked Salmon and Avocado Terrines

Line 4 ramekins with clingfilm. Divide 200 g (7 oz) thinly sliced smoked salmon between the ramekins, lining each dish and allowing plenty of overhang. Mix together 50 g (2 oz) soft goats' cheese, 2 tablespoons snipped chives, 2 peeled, stoned and chopped avocados and the juice of 1 lemon in a bowl and season to taste. Spoon the mixture into the dishes, then press down and fold over the salmon to cover. Cover and chill for 10–12 minutes. Turn out on to plates and serve with a green salad.

20 Hummus with Carrot and Celery Sticks

Serves 4

5 tablespoons extra virgin olive oil, plus extra for brushing
2 garlic cloves, crushed
40 g (1¾ oz) walnuts
400 g (13 oz) can chickpeas, rinsed and drained
1½ tablespoons tahini paste
juice of ½ lemon
½ tablespoon chopped coriander
salt and pepper

To serve

2 wholemeal pitta breads
2 tablespoons sesame seeds
2 large carrots, peeled and cut into batons
4 celery sticks, cut into batons

· Heat 4 tablespoons of the oil in a frying pan, add the garlic and cook for 2–3 minutes. Remove from the heat and leave to cool slightly.

· Heat a nonstick frying pan over a medium-low heat and dry-fry the walnuts for 3–4 minutes, stirring frequently, until slightly golden and giving off an aroma.

· Place the chickpeas, tahini, lemon juice, garlic oil and toasted walnuts in a food processor and process until smooth, adding a little water to loosen the mixture if necessary. Stir in the coriander and season to taste. Spoon into a bowl.

· Toast the pitta breads under a preheated medium grill for 4 minutes, then turn over, brush with the remaining oil and sprinkle with the sesame seeds. Toast until golden, then cut into strips.

· Serve the hummus with the pitta strips and the carrot and celery sticks.

---

1 Hummus and Carrot Wraps

Spread 200 g (7 oz) ready-made hummus over 4 seeded tortilla wraps. Peel and coarsely grate 4 carrots and sprinkle over the hummus. Top each one with a handful of rocket leaves, a small handful of coriander leaves and a sprinkling of lemon juice and olive oil. Roll up the wraps and serve.

3 Carrot and Haloumi Salad with Hummus Dressing Mix together 3 peeled and chopped carrots and 1 tablespoon olive oil in a roasting tin. Place in a preheated oven, 200°C (400°F), Gas Mark 6, for 20–25 minutes, adding 2 tablespoons walnut halves 5 minutes before the end of the cooking time. Meanwhile, sprinkle 250 g (8 oz) cubed haloumi cheese with ½ teaspoon dried oregano, then dry-fry in a nonstick frying pan for 2–3 minutes on each side until golden. Mix together 2 tablespoons ready-made hummus and 75 ml (3 fl oz) natural yogurt in a small bowl. Toss together the haloumi, roasted carrots and walnuts, 4 chopped tomatoes and 1 sliced red onion in a bowl. Place 50 g (2 oz) baby salad leaves on 4 plates, top with the carrot salad and serve drizzled with the hummus dressing.

Broccoli and Black-Eyed Bean Soup

Serves 4

2 tablespoons olive oil

2 large carrots, peeled and diced

8 spring onions, sliced

1.5 litres (2½ pints) hot
vegetable stock

300 g (10 oz) purple sprouting
broccoli, chopped

400 g (13 oz) can black-eyed
beans, rinsed and drained

For the croûtons

1 slice of crusty wholemeal bread

75 g (3 oz) goats' cheese

- Heat 1 tablespoon of the oil in a large saucepan, add the carrots and spring onions and sauté for 2–3 minutes. Pour in the stock and add the broccoli. Bring to the boil, then reduce the heat and simmer for 10 minutes until the broccoli is tender.

- Add the black-eyed beans and cook for a further 4–6 minutes until the beans are heated through.

- Meanwhile, make the croûtons. Toast the bread under a preheated hot grill for 2–3 minutes on each side, then top with the goats' cheese and grill until the cheese is bubbling. Cut into squares.

- Ladle the soup into bowls, then top with the croûtons and sprinkle over the remaining oil.

10 Broccoli and Black-Eyed Bean Salad

Cook 300 g (10 oz) broccoli florets in a saucepan of boiling water for 4–5 minutes, then drain, refresh under cold running water and drain again. Whisk together 3 tablespoons olive oil, 1 tablespoon balsamic vinegar, 1 teaspoon honey and 1 teaspoon Dijon mustard in a large bowl. Gently mix in the broccoli, a rinsed and drained 400 g (13 oz) can black-eyed beans, 1 sliced red onion, 175 g (6 oz) roasted red peppers from a jar, cut into strips, and 40 g (1¾ oz) watercress. Serve with crusty wholemeal bread.

30 Broccoli and Black-Eyed Bean Curry

Heat 2 tablespoons olive oil in a saucepan, add 1 large chopped onion and cook for 3–4 minutes until softened. Add 2 crushed garlic cloves, 1 tablespoon curry powder, 1 teaspoon ground cumin and 1 teaspoon turmeric and cook for a further 1–2 minutes. Stir in 50 g (2 oz) red split lentils, a rinsed and drained 400 g (13 oz) can black-eyed beans, 50 g (2 oz) raisins and 300 g (10 oz) broccoli florets. Pour in a 400 g (13 oz) can chopped tomatoes and 300 ml (½ pint) hot vegetable stock and bring to a simmer. Cook for 20–22 minutes, stirring occasionally. Serve with steamed basmati rice.

30 Smoked Haddock and Kale Soup

Serves 4

1 tablespoon olive oil
2 shallots, diced
3 garlic cloves, crushed
1 large potato, peeled and diced
350 ml (12 fl oz) soya milk
500 ml (17 fl oz) water
300 g (10 oz) kale, shredded
300 g (10 oz) smoked haddock,
　skinned and chopped
salt and pepper

- Heat the oil in a saucepan, add the shallots and garlic and cook for 3–4 minutes until softened. Add the potato, milk and measurement water and season to taste. Bring to the boil, then reduce the heat and simmer for 5–6 minutes.

- Stir in the kale and cook for a further 10–12 minutes until the vegetables are tender. Stir in the haddock and simmer for 2 minutes or until cooked through.

- Ladle the soup into bowls and serve immediately.

10 Spicy Smoked Haddock and Kale

Pasta Heat 4 tablespoons olive oil in a frying pan, add 2 deseeded and sliced red chillies, 3 sliced garlic cloves and 6 finely chopped anchovy fillets and cook for 1 minute. Stir in 400 g (13 oz) shredded kale and gently cook for 7–8 minutes until tender, adding a little water if necessary. Add 125 g (4 oz) skinned and chopped smoked haddock 4 minutes before the end of the cooking time. Meanwhile, cook 400 g (13 oz) fresh penne in a saucepan of boiling water for 4–5 minutes, or according to the pack instructions. Drain and toss with the kale, the juice of ½ lemon and 3 tablespoons grated Parmesan cheese. Serve sprinkled with 2 tablespoons Parmesan shavings.

20 Smoked Haddock Fishcakes with

Kale Cook 400 g (13 oz) smoked haddock under a preheated hot grill for 4 minutes on each side, then skin and flake into a large bowl. Mix in 625 g (1¼ lb) ready-made fresh mashed potatoes, 1 tablespoon chopped rinsed and drained capers, the grated rind of 1 lemon, 2 tablespoons chopped parsley and 1 beaten egg. Mix well, then shape into 8 fishcakes and dust with a little flour. Heat 2 tablespoons olive oil in a frying pan and cook the fishcakes for 3–4 minutes on each side until golden. Meanwhile, heat 2 tablespoons olive oil in a separate pan, add 250 g (8 oz) chopped kale and cook for 3–4 minutes until wilted. Serve with the fishcakes.

3 Roasted Butternut, Sage and Cashew Soup

Serves 4

1 kg (2 lb) butternut squash, peeled, deseeded and chopped into 1 cm (½ inch) chunks
2 tablespoons olive oil
1 tablespoon chopped sage
2 tablespoons pumpkin seeds
1 onion, chopped
1 garlic clove, chopped
½ tablespoon mild curry powder
2 tablespoons cashew nuts
600 ml (1 pint) hot vegetable stock
8 tablespoons natural yogurt
salt and pepper

- Place the butternut squash in a roasting tin and toss with 1 tablespoon of the oil and the sage. Place in a preheated oven, 220°C (425°F), Gas Mark 7, for 18–20 minutes until tender and golden.

- Meanwhile, heat a nonstick frying pan over a medium-low heat and dry-fry the pumpkin seeds for 2–3 minutes, stirring frequently, until golden brown and toasted. Set aside.

- Heat the remaining oil in a saucepan, add the onion and garlic and cook for 4–5 minutes until softened. Stir in the curry powder and cook for a further minute, stirring.

- Add the roasted squash, cashews and stock and bring to the boil, then reduce the heat and simmer for 3–4 minutes. Stir in the yogurt. Using a hand-held blender, blend the soup until smooth. Season to taste.

- Ladle the soup into bowls and serve sprinkled with the toasted pumpkin seeds.

1 Butternut, Sage and Cashew Dip

Cook 300 g (10 oz) peeled, deseeded and finely diced butternut squash in boiling water for 6–7 minutes until tender. Drain and cool for 1 minute. Meanwhile, dry-fry 100 g (3½ oz) cashew nuts until golden. Place in a food processor with 1 tablespoon tahini and 2 garlic cloves and blend until smooth. Add the squash, the juice of ½–1 lime, ½ tablespoon chopped sage and a pinch of chilli powder. Season, then blend with 1–2 tablespoons olive oil to the desired consistency.

2 Butternut and Sage Colcannon

Cook 750 g (1½ lb) peeled, deseeded and chopped butternut squash and 300 g (10 oz) peeled and chopped potatoes in a saucepan of boiling water for 12–15 minutes until tender. Meanwhile, cook ½ shredded savoy cabbage in a separate pan of boiling water for 4–5 minutes, then drain and keep warm. Bring a saucepan of water to a gentle simmer and stir with a large spoon to create a swirl. Break 2 eggs into the water and cook for 3 minutes. Remove with a slotted spoon and keep warm. Repeat with another 2 eggs. Drain the squash and potatoes, then mash in the pan with 1 tablespoon natural yogurt, 1 tablespoon chopped sage and 25 g (1 oz) butter. Season well and stir in the cabbage. Serve topped with the poached eggs.

20  Gazpacho

Serves 4

4 red peppers, cored, deseeded
    and roughly chopped
1 red onion, roughly chopped
2 cucumbers, roughly chopped
handful of basil leaves
handful of parsley leaves
2 garlic cloves
2 tablespoons sherry vinegar
    or balsamic vinegar
150 ml (¼ pint) olive oil
450 ml (¾ pint) chilled
    tomato juice
salt and pepper

To serve

1 avocado, peeled, stoned and
    chopped
1 soft-boiled egg, quartered

- Place the vegetables, herbs and garlic in the food processor and process until finely chopped.

- Add the remaining ingredients, season to taste and process again briefly. Cover and chill for 5 minutes.

- Serve in bowls topped with the chopped avocados and quartered eggs.

---

10 Mediterranean Pepper Salad

Bring a saucepan of water to a gentle simmer and stir with a large spoon to create a swirl. Break 2 eggs into the water and cook for 3 minutes. Remove with a slotted spoon and keep warm. Repeat with another 2 eggs. Toss together 50 g (2 oz) watercress, 1 sliced red onion, ½ chopped cucumber, 2 peeled, stoned and sliced avocados, 10–12 basil leaves and a small handful of parsley leaves in a serving bowl. Cut 4 roasted red pepper from a jar into slices. Top the salad with the peppers and poached eggs, then drizzle with salad dressing.

30 Red Pepper Tarts

Unroll a 375 g (12 oz) pack ready-rolled puff pastry and cut into 4 rectangles. Place on a baking sheet and top each with ½ peeled, stoned and mashed avocado, 2–3 basil leaves, ½ sliced tomato and 100 g (3½ oz) sliced roasted red peppers from a jar. Sprinkle with 2 tablespoons pine nuts and 2 tablespoons grated Parmesan cheese. Bake in a preheated oven, 200°C (400°F), Gas Mark 6, for 20 minutes until the pastry is golden. Serve with rocket salad.

Warm Lentil, Tomato and Haloumi Salad

Serves 4

250 g (8 oz) haloumi cheese,
  cut into chunks
½ red onion, sliced
250 g (8 oz) cherry tomatoes,
  halved
400 g (13 oz) can lentils, rinsed
  and drained
1 garlic clove, crushed
juice of ½ lemon
2 tablespoons extra virgin
  olive oil
small handful of coriander leaves,
  roughly chopped
small handful of mint leaves,
  roughly chopped

- Heat a nonstick frying pan over a medium heat and dry-fry the haloumi for 4–5 minutes, turning frequently, until golden.

- Meanwhile, toss together the remaining ingredients in a bowl. Stir in the cooked haloumi and serve immediately.

---

2 Lentil and Tomato Soup

Heat 1 tablespoon olive oil in a saucepan, add 1 chopped onion, 2 peeled and chopped carrots and 2 sliced celery sticks and cook for 5–6 minutes. Add 1 crushed garlic clove, 1 teaspoon ground cumin and 175 g (6 oz) red split lentils. Pour in 1.2 litres (2 pints) hot vegetable stock, a 400 g (13 oz) can chopped tomatoes and 2 teaspoons tomato purée and bring to the boil, then simmer for 15–17 minutes until the lentils are cooked. Using a hand-held blender, blend the soup until smooth, then season. Serve with swirls of natural yogurt, sprinkled with chopped coriander.

3 Lentil and Tomato Flatbreads

Mix together 875 g (1¾ lb) self-raising flour and 100 g (3½ oz) baking powder in a bowl, add 400 g (13 oz) diced chilled butter and rub in with the fingertips until the mixture resembles fine breadcrumbs. Add a rinsed and drained 400 g (13 oz) can lentils, 400 ml (14 fl oz) milk and 1 teaspoon salt and mix well. Using your hands, roughly shape the mixture into 4 x 23-cm (9-inch) rounds. Place on a baking sheet and top with 2 thinly sliced tomatoes, a small handful of roughly torn basil leaves and a drizzle of olive oil. Bake in a preheated oven, 200°C (400°F), Gas Mark 6, for 15–20 minutes.

10 Peach, Feta and Watercress Salad

Serves 4

30 g (1 oz) pumpkin seeds
juice of ½ lemon
2 tablespoons extra virgin olive oil
½ teaspoon Dijon mustard
1 teaspoon honey
1 tablespoon chopped oregano
75 g (3 oz) watercress
3 peaches, halved, stoned and
    sliced
4 spring onions, sliced
175 g (6 oz) feta cheese,
    crumbled
pepper

- Heat a nonstick frying pan over a medium-low heat and dry-fry the pumpkin seeds for 2–3 minutes, stirring frequently, until slightly golden and toasted. Set aside.

- Whisk together the lemon juice, oil, mustard, honey, oregano and pepper in a small bowl.

- Divide the watercress between 4 plates, top with the peach slices and spring onions, then sprinkle over the feta cheese.

- Serve sprinkled with the toasted pumpkin seeds and drizzled with the dressing.

20 Peach, Feta and Watercress Bruschetta

Cut 2 baguettes into 1.5 cm (¾ inch) slices. Place the slices on a baking sheet and drizzle with 2 tablespoons olive oil. Bake in a preheated oven, 200°C (400°F), Gas Mark 6, for 10–12 minutes until golden. Rub one side of each slice with a garlic clove. Halve, stone and slice 4 peaches. Top the toasts with a few sprigs of watercress, the peach slices and 125 g (4 oz) crumbled feta cheese. Serve drizzled with balsamic glaze.

30 Roasted Feta-Topped Peach and Watercress Salad

Halve and stone 4 peaches and place in a roasting tin. Sprinkle with 200 g (7 oz) crumbled feta cheese, 1 tablespoon olive oil and 1 teaspoon cumin seeds. Season with pepper. Place in a preheated oven, 200°C (400°F), Gas Mark 6, for 15–18 minutes until the peaches are soft and the cheese is melted. Meanwhile, whisk together 3 tablespoons olive oil, 1 tablespoon balsamic vinegar, ½ teaspoon wholegrain mustard and ½ teaspoon caster sugar in a small bowl. Divide 75 g (3 oz) watercress between 4 shallow bowls and sprinkle over 1 small diced red onion and 100 g (3½ oz) quartered cherry tomatoes. Top with the roasted peach halves. Pour any juices from the tin into the dressing and whisk together, then drizzle over the salad to serve.

 # Avocado, Pepper and Olive Salad

Serves 4

1 tablespoon sesame seeds
2 avocados, peeled, stoned
  and chopped
juice of 1 lime
1 red pepper, cored, deseeded
  and chopped
1 yellow pepper, cored, deseeded
  and chopped
½ cucumber, finely chopped
2 carrots, peeled and chopped
2 tomatoes, chopped
4 spring onions, sliced
10 pitted black olives, halved
1 romaine lettuce, roughly torn
4 tablespoons salad dressing
1 tablespoon chopped mint

- Heat a nonstick frying pan over a medium-low heat and dry-fry the sesame seeds for 2 minutes, stirring frequently, until golden brown and toasted. Set aside.

- Meanwhile, place the avocados in a large bowl and toss with the lime juice to prevent discoloration. Gently toss together with the remaining ingredients except the sesame seeds.

- Sprinkle the salad with the toasted sesame seeds and serve.

---

2 Haloumi with Avocado, Pepper and Olive Salsa Halve, core and deseed 2 red peppers and cook, skin side up, under a preheated hot grill for 10–12 minutes until blackened. Place in a bowl, cover with clingfilm and leave to cool for 5 minutes. Meanwhile, slice 250 g (8 oz) haloumi cheese and dry-fry in a nonstick frying pan for 3–4 minutes on each side until golden. Peel the skin from the red peppers, then cut into slices. Place 150 g (5 oz) baby spinach leaves on a serving plate, top with 2 sliced beef tomatoes, 6 sliced spring onions, 2 peeled, stoned and sliced avocados, the haloumi slices and 12–16 pitted black olives. Serve drizzled with salad dressing.

3 Peperonata with Avocado and Olives Heat 3 tablespoons olive oil in a frying pan, add 2 sliced garlic cloves and 3 sliced onions and cook for 1–2 minutes. Core, deseed and slice 2 red peppers and 2 yellow peppers, then add to the pan and cook for 10 minutes. Add 350 g (11½ oz) chopped ripe tomatoes and cook for a further 12–15 minutes until the peppers are soft. Stir in 1 peeled, stoned and chopped avocado, 12 halved pitted black olives and a small handful of basil leaves. Serve with crusty bread.

Salmon and Chickpea Salad

Serves 4

625 g (1¼ lb) salmon fillet, skinned
1 orange
grated rind of ½ lemon
2 tablespoons extra virgin olive oil
400 g (13 oz) can chickpeas,
   rinsed and drained
60 g (2¼ oz) watercress
2 tablespoons caper berries,
   rinsed and drained
small handful of mint leaves,
   roughly torn
salt and pepper

· Cook the salmon under a preheated hot grill for 8–9 minutes, turning once, or until cooked through.

· Meanwhile, grate the rind of the orange into a bowl, then peel and segment the orange, catching the juice in the bowl. Whisk together the orange juice and rind, grated lemon rind, oil and salt and pepper.

· Flake the salmon in large pieces into a serving bowl. Toss together with the remaining ingredients, the orange segments and dressing, then serve.

---

2 Grilled Salmon with Chickpea Curry

Heat 1 tablespoon olive oil in a saucepan, add 1 chopped onion, 1 tablespoon peeled and grated fresh root ginger and 2 crushed garlic cloves, and cook for 1–2 minutes. Stir in 1 teaspoon each of ground cumin, ground coriander, turmeric and chilli powder, then add 3 chopped tomatoes and 2 rinsed and drained 400 g (13 oz) cans chickpeas. Pour in 150 ml (¼ pint) water and simmer for 12–14 minutes. Stir in 2 tablespoons chopped coriander. Meanwhile, cook 4 salmon fillets, about 150 g (5 oz) each, under a preheated hot grill for 4–5 minutes on each side. Serve with the curry.

3 Salmon en Papillote with Warm Chickpea Salad

Toss 2 red onions, cut into wedges, with 1 tablespoon olive oil in roasting tin. Place in a preheated oven, 200°C (400°F), Gas Mark 6, for 25 minutes. Meanwhile, place 4 skinless salmon fillets, about 150 g (5 oz) each, in the centre of 4 squares of greaseproof paper and add ½ tablespoon olive oil, a splash of white wine and a few coriander sprigs to each. Fold up to make parcels and place on a baking sheet. Bake in the oven for 6–8 minutes or until cooked through. While the fish is cooking, cook 300 g (10 oz) broccoli florets in a saucepan of boiling water for 4–5 minutes until tender, then drain, refresh under cold running water and drain again. Heat a rinsed and drained 400 g (13 oz) can chickpeas in a pan until warmed through, then toss with the red onion and broccoli. Serve the salmon parcels with the warm salad.

1 Warm Smoked Duck and Asparagus Salad

Serves 4

2 smoked duck breasts, sliced
350 g (11½ oz) asparagus, trimmed
20 radishes, quartered
2 tablespoons walnut pieces
3 tablespoons olive oil
1 tablespoon balsamic vinegar
3 shop-bought ready-cooked fresh beetroot, diced

- Cook the duck in a dry frying pan for 3–4 minutes until the fat is released. Remove from the pan using a slotted spoon and keep warm.

- Meanwhile, cook the asparagus in a saucepan of boiling water for 2–3 minutes, then drain and halve widthways. Add to the fat in the frying pan and cook for 1–2 minutes until lightly browned, then stir in the radishes and cook for 1 minute.

- While the asparagus is cooking, heat a nonstick frying pan over a medium-low heat and dry-fry the walnuts for 3–4 minutes, stirring frequently, until slightly golden. Whisk together the oil and vinegar in a bowl.

- Toss together the duck, asparagus and radishes, toasted walnuts and beetroot. Serve drizzled with the dressing.

2 Pan-Fried Duck Breasts with Griddled Asparagus

Using a sharp knife, make 3 slashes through the skin of 4 duck breasts. Rub each one with ¼ teaspoon Chinese five spice powder. Heat ½ tablespoon olive oil in a large frying pan until very hot, then add the duck, skin side down, and cook for 8–10 minutes until the skin is crisp and brown. Tip out the excess fat and add 2 star anise to the pan. Turn the duck over and cook for a further 5 minutes, or until cooked to your liking. Meanwhile, toss 300 g (10 oz) trimmed asparagus with 1 tablespoon olive oil, then cook in a preheated hot griddle pan for 3–4 minutes, turning once. Remove the duck from the pan and leave to rest for 2–3 minutes. Add 4 chopped spring onions, 2 tablespoons soy sauce, 100 ml (3½ fl oz) chicken stock and 2 teaspoons honey to the duck pan and simmer for 2 minutes. Serve the duck with the sauce and asparagus.

3 Smoked Duck and Asparagus Tarts

Cook 300 g (10 oz) trimmed asparagus in a saucepan of boiling water for 2 minutes, then drain. Unroll a 375 g (12 oz) pack ready-rolled puff pastry and cut into 4 rectangles. Place on a baking sheet and spread each one with 2 tablespoons cream cheese, leaving a 1.5 cm (¾ inch) border. Top with the asparagus and 1 sliced smoked duck breast. Season with pepper and drizzle with 1 tablespoon olive oil. Cook in a preheated oven, 200°C (400°F), Gas Mark 6, for 20–25 minutes until golden. Serve sprinkled with Parmesan cheese shavings.

30 Smoked Mackerel Superfood Salad

Serves 4

500 g (1 lb) butternut squash, peeled, deseeded and cut into 1 cm (½ inch) cubes

4 tablespoons olive oil

1 teaspoon cumin seeds

1 head of broccoli, cut into florets

200 g (7 oz) frozen or fresh peas

3 tablespoons quinoa

4 tablespoons mixed seeds

2 smoked mackerel fillets

juice of 1 lemon

½ teaspoon honey

½ teaspoon Dijon mustard

100 g (3½ oz) red cabbage, shredded

4 tomatoes, chopped

4 cooked beetroot, cut into wedges

20 g (¾ oz) radish sprouts

· Place the squash in a roasting tin and sprinkle with 1 tablespoon of the olive oil and the cumin seeds. Place in a preheated oven, 200°C (400°F), Gas Mark 6, for 15–18 minutes until tender. Leave to cool slightly.

· Meanwhile, cook the broccoli in boiling water for 4–5 minutes until tender, adding the peas 3 minutes before the end of the cooking time. Remove with a slotted spoon and refresh under cold running water, then drain. Cook the quinoa in the broccoli water for 15 minutes, then drain and leave to cool slightly.

· Heat a nonstick frying pan over a medium-low heat and dry-fry the seeds, stirring frequently, until golden brown and toasted. Set aside. Heat the mackerel fillets according to the pack instructions, then skin and break into flakes.

· Whisk together the remaining olive oil, lemon juice, honey and mustard in a small bowl. Toss together all the ingredients, except the radish sprouts, with the dressing in a serving bowl. Serve topped with the sprouts.

---

10 Smoked Mackerel Superfood Toasts

Mash together the flesh of 2 peeled and stoned avocados, 1 crushed garlic clove, the juice of ½ lime and 2 chopped tomatoes in a bowl. Toast 4 slices of granary bread under a preheated hot grill for 2–3 minutes on each side, then spread one side of each slice with 1 teaspoon creamed horseradish. Top each with 15 g (½ oz) watercress, 1 sliced small ready-cooked fresh beetroot and ½ skinned and flaked smoked mackerel fillet. Top with the avocado mixture, a sprinkling of pumpkin seeds, toasted as above, and a small handful of alfalfa sprouts.

20 Smoked Mackerel Superfood Soup

Heat 1 tablespoon oil in a saucepan and fry 1 chopped onion and 1 crushed garlic clove for 3–4 minutes. Add 625 g (1¼ lb) peeled, deseeded and diced butternut squash, 100 g (3½ oz) broccoli florets, 2 tablespoons quinoa, 600 ml (1 pint) vegetable stock and 150 ml (¼ pint) orange juice and simmer for 15 minutes. Blend until smooth. Stir in 2 skinned, flaked smoked mackerel fillets and cook for 1 minute. Serve sprinkled with 2 tablespoons toasted pumpkin seeds.

HEA-SNAC-KUH

 # Beetroot and Goats' Cheese Salad

Serves 4

2 tablespoons olive oil

3 raw beetroot, peeled and grated

4 tablespoons balsamic vinegar

2 tablespoons sunflower seeds

200 g (7 oz) goats' cheese

75 g (3 oz) rocket leaves

2 tablespoons extra virgin olive oil

pepper

- Heat the olive oil in a frying pan, add the beetroot and cook for 3–4 minutes. Season well with pepper, then stir in the vinegar and cook over a high heat for 30 seconds.

- Meanwhile, heat a nonstick frying pan over a medium-low heat and dry-fry the sunflower seeds for 2 minutes, stirring frequently, until golden and toasted. Set aside.

- Divide the beetroot between 4 plates. Crumble over the cheese and top with the rocket.

- Serve drizzled with the extra virgin olive oil and sprinkled with the toasted sunflower seeds.

2 Beetroot Soup with Goats' Cheese

Heat 1 tablespoon olive oil in a saucepan, add 1 chopped onion and cook for 2–3 minutes. Add 3 grated raw beetroot, 600 ml (1 pint) hot vegetable stock and a 400 g (13 oz) can chopped tomatoes and bring to the boil. Reduce the heat and simmer for 8–10 minutes until the beetroot is tender. Using a hand-held blender, blend the soup until smooth, then season to taste. Ladle into bowls and crumble over 100 g (3½ oz) goats' cheese to serve.

3 Roasted Beetroot and Goats' Cheese Salad

Place 200 g (7 oz) halved raw baby beetroot and 200 g (7 oz) halved baby carrots in a roasting tin, sprinkle with 2 tablespoons cumin seeds and drizzle with 2 tablespoons olive oil. Place in a preheated oven, 200°C (400°F), Gas Mark 6, for 20–25 minutes. Meanwhile, dry-fry 2 tablespoons walnuts in a nonstick frying pan for 3–4 minutes, stirring frequently, until slightly golden. Set aside. Mix together 3 tablespoons olive oil, the juice of ½ lemon, 1 teaspoon wholegrain mustard and 1 teaspoon honey in a small bowl. Place 200 g (7 oz) salad leaves on a large serving plate. Cook 4 x 100 g (3½ oz) slices of goats' cheese under a preheated medium-hot grill for 4–5 minutes until golden. Toss together the roasted vegetables, dressing and salad leaves and divide between 4 plates. Top with the grilled goats' cheese and sprinkle with the toasted walnuts.

Mini Smoked Trout Quiches

Serves 4

½ tablespoon rapeseed oil
400 g (13 oz) baby spinach leaves
6 large eggs
100 ml (3½ fl oz) milk
3 tablespoons Parmesan cheese,
  grated
2 tablespoons finely chopped
  chives
150 g (5 oz) hot-smoked trout
  fillets, flaked
4 cherry tomatoes, halved
salt and pepper

- Line 8 holes of a muffin tin with 15 cm (6 inch) squares of greaseproof paper.

- Heat the oil in a frying pan, add the spinach and cook briefly until wilted. Remove from the heat.

- Beat together the eggs, milk and cheese in a jug and season to taste, then stir in the chives and trout.

- Divide the spinach between the muffin cases, then pour in the egg mixture. Top each one with half a tomato.

- Bake in a preheated oven, 180°C (350°F), Gas Mark 4, for 12–15 minutes until just set.

---

1 **Smoked Trout Baked Eggs**

Brush 4 ramekins with melted butter, then add 50 g (2 oz) flaked hot-smoked trout fillet to each dish. Carefully break 2 eggs into each ramekin, top with 2 tablespoons grated Cheddar cheese and season. Place the ramekins in a roasting tin with enough boiling water to come three-quarters of the way up the sides of the dishes. Bake in a preheated oven, 200°C (400°F), Gas Mark 6, for 8–9 minutes until the cheese has melted and the egg is cooked but still soft. Serve with toast.

3 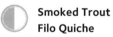 **Smoked Trout Filo Quiche**

Heat 25 g (1 oz) butter in a frying pan, add 1 trimmed and sliced leek and cook for 2–3 minutes. Meanwhile, lay 1 sheet of filo pastry in a 23-cm (9-inch) fluted tart tin and fold over any overhang. Repeat with another sheet to cover the base, then brush with melted butter. Repeat with a further 6 sheets, turning the tin to ensure all sides are covered with pastry. Sprinkle the pastry base with 350 g (11½ oz) grated Cheddar cheese and 200 g (7 oz) flaked hot-smoked trout fillets, then

add the leeks. Beat together 3 eggs, 125 ml (4 fl oz) double cream and 125 ml (4 fl oz) natural yogurt, then pour into the case. Top with 2 sliced tomatoes. Bake in a preheated oven, 190°C (375°F), Gas Mark 5, for 25 minutes until golden.

Rosemary Oatcakes

Makes 20-24

200 g (7 oz) rolled oats

3 rosemary sprigs, leaves stripped

125 g (4 oz) plain flour, plus extra for dusting

¾ teaspoon baking powder

pinch of salt

75 g (3 oz) chilled unsalted butter, diced

100 ml (3½ fl oz) milk

- Place the oats and rosemary in a food processor and process until they resemble breadcrumbs. Add the flour, baking powder and salt and blitz again. Add the butter, then process until it is mixed in. With the motor still running, pour in the milk through the feed tube until the dough forms a ball.

- Turn the dough out on to a floured surface and roll out to about 4–5 mm (¼ inch) thick. Cut out 20–24 rounds using a 5–6 cm (2–2½ inch) plain biscuit cutter, re-rolling the trimmings as necessary.

- Place on a baking sheet and bake in a preheated oven, 190°C (375°F), Gas Mark 5, for 12–15 minutes until golden at the edges. Transfer to a wire rack to cool. Store in an airtight container.

---

1 **Mixed Salad with Rosemary Dressing**

Whisk together 1 tablespoon balsamic vinegar, 3 tablespoons olive oil, 2 teaspoons Dijon mustard, 1 teaspoon finely chopped rosemary and 1 teaspoon honey in a small bowl and season with salt and pepper. Toss together 200 g (7 oz) green salad leaves, 1 cored, deseeded and chopped yellow pepper, 1 sliced red onion and the dressing in a serving bowl. Serve with grilled fish or chicken.

2 **Rosemary Scones**

Sift together 225 g (7½ oz) self-raising flour, 1 teaspoon baking powder and a pinch of salt and black pepper in a bowl. Add 40 g (1¾ oz) diced chilled butter and rub in with the fingertips until the mixture resembles fine breadcrumbs. Stir in 1½ tablespoons chopped rosemary and 50 g (2 oz) grated Cheddar cheese. Add 150 ml (¼ pint) milk and mix with a palette knife to a soft dough. Turn out on to a lightly floured surface and press or roll out to 1.5 cm (¾ inch) thick. Cut out 12 rounds using a 4–5 cm (1½–2 inch) cutter, re-rolling the trimmings as necessary, and place on a baking sheet. Sprinkle the tops with 50 g (2 oz) grated Cheddar. Bake in a preheated oven, 220°C (425°F), Gas Mark 7, for 8–10 minutes until golden. Transfer to a wire rack to cool.

Wholemeal Cheese Straws

Makes 12–16

100 g (3½ oz) wholemeal plain flour, plus extra for dusting

2 teaspoons paprika

150 g (5 oz) mature Cheddar cheese, grated

100 g (3½ oz) chilled unsalted butter, diced

2 teaspoons baking powder

2 egg yolks

- Mix together the flour and paprika in a bowl, then stir in the cheese. Add the butter and rub in with the fingertips until the mixture resembles fine breadcrumbs. Stir in the baking powder, then add the egg yolks and mix to a stiff dough.

- Turn the dough out on to a floured surface and press or roll out to about 5 mm (¼ inch) thick. Cut into 1 cm (½ inch) wide straws and place on a baking sheet.

- Bake in a preheated oven, 220°C (425°F), Gas Mark 7, for 10–12 minutes until golden. Transfer to a wire rack to cool.

Cheese and Pickle Toasts

Toast 4 slices of thick granary bread under a preheated hot grill for 2–3 minutes on each side. Meanwhile, mix together 200 g (7 oz) grated Cheddar cheese, 4 sliced spring onions and 2 diced tomatoes in a bowl. Spread one side of each toast with 1 tablespoon pickle, then spoon over the cheese mixture and grill for a further 2–3 minutes until bubbling and golden.

Cheese Soda Bread

Sift together 450 g (14½ oz) plain flour and 1 teaspoon bicarbonate of soda in a bowl. Stir in 1 teaspoon salt and 50 g (2 oz) grated Cheddar cheese. Make a well in the centre and pour in 400 ml (14 fl oz) buttermilk. Using your hands, mix together to form a soft dough. Turn the dough out on to a floured surface and roll out to 35 x 20 cm (14 x 8 inches). Transfer to an oiled baking sheet and brush the top with 1 tablespoon olive oil. Sprinkle with 75 g (3 oz) grated Cheddar cheese and bake in a preheated oven, 220°C (425°F), Gas Mark 7, for 10 minutes, then reduce the temperature to 200°C (400°F), Gas Mark 6, and cook for a further 8–12 minutes until golden and firm. Transfer to a wire rack to cool. Serve cut into squares.

 # Cheese, Cumin and Apple Scones

Makes about 10

125 g (4 oz) self-raising flour, plus extra for dusting

100 g (3½ oz) wholemeal self-raising flour

40 g (1¾ oz) chilled butter, diced, plus extra to serve

1 teaspoon cumin seeds

75 g (3 oz) Cheddar cheese, grated

1 dessert apple, peeled, cored and diced

150 ml (¼ pint) milk

chutney, to serve

- Sift the flours into a large bowl, add the butter and rub in with the fingertips until the mixture resembles fine breadcrumbs. Stir in the cumin seeds, two-thirds of the cheese and the apple, then add the milk and mix with a palette knife to a soft dough.

- Turn the dough out on to a floured surface and press out to 1.5 cm (¾ inch) thick. Cut out about 10 rounds using a 5 cm (2 inch) plain biscuit cutter or glass, using the trimmings as necessary.

- Place the scones on a baking sheet and sprinkle with the remaining cheese. Bake in a preheated oven, 220°C (425°F), Gas Mark 7, for 15–18 minutes until risen and golden. Transfer to a wire rack to cool or serve warm, spread with butter and chutney.

1 Cheese, Cumin and Apple Toasts

Toast 4 slices of granary bread under a preheated hot grill for 2–3 minutes on each side. Spread one side of each slice with 2 teaspoons chutney. Core and thinly slice 2 dessert apples and arrange over the toasts. Sprinkle with ½ teaspoon cumin seeds, then top each one with 75 g (3 oz) grated Cheddar cheese. Grill for a further 1–2 minutes until the cheese is bubbling and golden. Serve with a crisp green salad.

2 Cheese, Cumin and Apple Salad

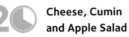

Dry-fry 50 g (2 oz) walnut pieces in a nonstick frying pan for 3–4 minutes, stirring frequently, until slightly golden. Set aside. Whisk together 4 tablespoons natural yogurt, 1 tablespoon lemon juice and ½ teaspoon ground cumin in a small bowl. In a separate bowl, mix together 3 cored and sliced apples, 2 sliced celery sticks, 50 g (2 oz) raisins and 60 g (2¼ oz) watercress. Add the yogurt dressing and toss until the salad is coated. Cook 4 x 100 g (3½ oz) slices of goats' cheese under a preheated medium-hot grill for 4–5 minutes or until golden. Divide the salad between 4 plates or shallow bowls and top each one with a goats' cheese slice. Serve sprinkled with the toasted walnuts.

# Mediterranean Beans

Serves 4

2 tablespoons extra virgin olive oil
1 red onion, diced
1 garlic clove, crushed
½ teaspoon cumin seeds
400 g (13 oz) can cannellini beans,
   rinsed and drained
75 g (3 oz) cherry tomatoes,
   quartered
2 teaspoons chopped sage
4 slices of crusty bread
salt and pepper
25 g (1 oz) Manchego cheese,
   grated, to serve

- Heat the oil in a large frying pan, add the onion and cook for 1–2 minutes. Add the garlic and cumin seeds and cook for a further 2–3 minutes.

- Add the beans and mix well to allow them to soak up the flavours, then add the tomatoes. Stir in the sage, season with salt and pepper and heat through.

- Meanwhile, toast the bread under a preheated hot grill for 2–3 minutes on each side. Serve topped with the beans and a sprinkling of cheese.

2 Bean and Garlic Stew

Heat 2 tablespoons olive oil in a large saucepan, add 1 large chopped onion and cook for 1–2 minutes. Add 2 peeled and thinly sliced carrots, 2 sliced celery sticks and 7–8 sliced garlic cloves and cook for a further 3 minutes. Add 2 rinsed and drained 400 g (13 oz) cans cannellini beans, ½ thickly shredded cabbage and 900 ml (1½ pints) hot vegetable stock and season well, then bring to a simmer and cook for 12–15 minutes, stirring in 3 tablespoons ground almonds 2 minutes before the end of the cooking time.

3 Mixed Bean Goulash

Heat 1 tablespoon olive oil in a large frying pan, add 1 large chopped onion and 2 crushed garlic cloves and gently fry for 5 minutes until softened. Stir in 100 g (3½ oz) chopped chestnut mushrooms and cook for a further 3–4 minutes. Add 1 tablespoon smoked paprika and continue to cook for 1–2 minutes. Stir in a 400 g (13 oz) can chopped tomatoes, 200 ml (7 fl oz) hot vegetable stock and a rinsed and drained 400 g (13 oz) can mixed beans and bring to the boil, then reduce the heat and simmer

for 12–14 minutes until thick and glossy. Serve with cooked rice, topped with dollops of soured cream, if liked.

Chorizo and Olive Tapenade Toasts

Serves 4

1 baguette, cut into 8 thick slices
1 garlic clove, chopped
200 g (7 oz) Kalamata olives, pitted
25 g (1 oz) anchovy fillets, drained
1 tablespoon capers, rinsed and drained
1 teaspoon chopped thyme
3 tablespoons lemon juice
4 tablespoons extra virgin olive oil
16 slices of chorizo

- Toast the bread under a preheated hot grill for 2–3 minutes on each side.

- Meanwhile, place the garlic, olives, anchovies, capers, thyme and lemon juice in a food processor or blender and blitz until combined. With the motor still running, slowly pour in the oil through the feed tube until the mixture forms a paste.

- Top each slice of toast with 2 slices of chorizo, then spoon the olive tapenade on top.

Chorizo and Olive Potatoes

Cook 875 g (1¾ lb) peeled and chopped potatoes in a saucepan of boiling water for 15 minutes until tender. Meanwhile, bring a saucepan of water to a gentle simmer and stir with a large spoon to create a swirl. Break 2 eggs into the water and cook for 3 minutes. Remove with a slotted spoon and keep warm. Repeat with another 2 eggs. Drain the potatoes, then mix with 100 g (3½ oz) chopped pitted black olives, 100 g (3½ oz) chopped chorizo and 2 tablespoons olive oil. Season, then lightly crush with a fork. Serve topped with the poached eggs.

Chorizo, Onion and Olive Tart

Heat 1 tablespoon olive oil in a frying pan, add 2 large red onions, cut into wedges, and cook for 5 minutes until softened. Stir in 2 tablespoons light brown sugar and 2 tablespoons balsamic vinegar and cook for a further 5 minutes. Leave to cool for 2 minutes. Unroll a 375 g (12 oz) pack ready-rolled puff pastry and place on a baking sheet. Score a 1 cm (½ inch) border around the outside, then spread the onion mixture within the border. Top with 10–12 slices of chorizo, then sprinkle with 100 g (3½ oz) crumbled goats' cheese and 175 g (6 oz) chopped pitted black olives. Season and drizzle with 1 tablespoon olive oil. Bake in a preheated oven, 220°C (425°F), Gas Mark 7, for 15 minutes until golden. Serve with a crisp green salad.

 Griddled Courgette Bruschetta

Serves 4

2 courgettes
1 tablespoon olive oil
150 g (5 oz) button mushrooms
8–10 slices of wholemeal or rye bread, ideally from a baguette
1 garlic clove
4 tablespoons canned chopped tomatoes
pepper

- Heat a griddle pan until very hot. Using a vegetable peeler, slice the courgettes into long, thin strips.

- Brush the hot griddle with the oil, add the courgette slices, in batches, and cook until charred with griddle marks. Remove from the pan and keep warm.

- Place the mushrooms in the griddle pan and cook for them 3–4 minutes, until softened.

- Meanwhile, toast the bread under a preheated hot grill for 2–3 minutes on each side, then rub one side of each slice with the garlic clove.

- Spread the toasts with a little chopped tomato, then divide the courgette strips and mushrooms between them. Season with pepper and serve.

1 **Quick Courgette Pasta**

Cook 400 g (13 oz) farfalle pasta in a saucepan of boiling water according to the pack instructions until 'al dente'. Meanwhile, heat 2 tablespoons olive oil in a large frying pan, add 3 large coarsely grated courgettes, 2 crushed garlic cloves and 1 deseeded and diced red chilli and cook for 5–6 minutes until softened. Drain the pasta, stir into the courgette mixture and toss together. Add a squeeze of lemon juice, season with pepper and serve sprinkled with grated Parmesan cheese.

3 **Courgette Lasagne**

Heat 1 tablespoon olive oil in a frying pan, add 1 chopped onion and cook for 2–3 minutes, then add 6 coarsely grated courgettes and 2 crushed garlic cloves and cook for a further 2–3 minutes. Stir in 200 g (7 oz) ricotta cheese and 20 g (¾ oz) grated Cheddar cheese. Heat 350 g (11½ oz) ready-made tomato sauce in a microwave. Cook 10 lasagne sheets in a saucepan of boiling water for 5 minutes until softened, then drain. Layer the courgette mixture, pasta and tomato sauce in an ovenproof dish, finishing with a layer of lasagne. Dot with 50 g (2 oz) ricotta and sprinkle with 40 g (1¾ oz) grated Cheddar. Bake in a preheated oven, 220°C (425°F), Gas Mark 7, for 10 minutes until golden.

Spiced Tuna Open Sandwiches

Serves 4

2 x 250 g (8 oz) cans tuna, drained
4 tablespoons mayonnaise
2 tablespoons sliced celery
¼ teaspoon smoked paprika
¼ teaspoon cayenne pepper
1 tablespoon finely chopped
  red onion
juice of ½ lemon
¼ cucumber, thinly sliced
4 slices of pumpernickel bread
a few sprigs of watercress
lemon wedges, to serve

- Flake the tuna in a bowl, then mix together with the mayonnaise, celery, paprika, cayenne pepper, onion and lemon juice.

- Arrange the slices of cucumber on the pumpernickel, then top with the tuna mixture. Top with a few sprigs of watercress.

- Serve with lemon wedges.

---

2 Spiced Tuna Salad Niçoise

Dust a 400 g (13 oz) tuna steak with 2 teaspoons each of ground cumin and ground coriander. Leave to stand for 10 minutes. Heat 1 tablespoon olive oil in an ovenproof frying pan until hot, add the tuna and cook for 30 seconds on each side until browned, then transfer to a preheated oven, 220°C (425°F), Gas Mark 7, for 5–6 minutes, or until cooked to your liking. Leave to rest. Meanwhile, using a pestle and mortar, pound together ½ garlic clove, 50 g (2 oz) can anchovy fillets in oil, drained, and 1 egg yolk. Add the juice of ½ lemon, 4–5 tablespoons olive oil and 1 teaspoon Dijon mustard and mix well. Set aside. Cook 275 g (9 oz) halved new potatoes in a saucepan of boiling water for 12 minutes, adding 125 g (4 oz) French beans 3–4 minutes before the end of the cooking time. Drain. Meanwhile, hard-boil 4 eggs in a separate pan of boiling water, then refresh under cold running water, peel and cut in half. Place the potatoes, beans and eggs in a bowl, flake the tuna and place on top. Pour over the dressing and serve.

3 Spicy Tuna Pasta Bake

Cook 400 g (13 oz) rigatoni in boiling water for 8–9 minutes. Meanwhile, melt 50 g (2 oz) butter in a saucepan, then stir in 50 g (2 oz) plain flour. Cook for 1–2 minutes, then gradually whisk in 600 ml (1 pint) milk and cook, stirring, until thick and smooth. Remove from the heat and stir in 1 teaspoon mustard and 125 g (4 oz) grated Cheddar cheese. Drain the pasta and mix with the sauce, a drained 340 g (12 oz) can sweetcorn, 2 drained 185 g (6½ oz) cans tuna, 1 teaspoon chilli flakes and a handful of chopped parsley. Season. Spoon into an ovenproof dish and top with 125 g (4 oz) grated Cheddar. Bake in a preheated oven, 200°C (400°F), Gas Mark 6, for 15 minutes.

Spicy Barbecue Beans on Toast

Serves 4

1 tablespoon olive oil

1 red onion, diced

2 garlic cloves, chopped

1 tablespoon red wine vinegar

1 tablespoon dark muscovado
   sugar

400 g (13 oz) can cannellini beans,
   rinsed and drained

1 tablespoon raisins

2 tablespoons flaked almonds

400 ml (14 fl oz) passata

1 teaspoon Worcestershire sauce

2 tablespoons chopped parsley

4 thick slices of granary bread

salt and pepper

2 tablespoons grated Manchego
   cheese, to serve

- Heat the oil in a saucepan, add the onion and fry for 3–4 minutes until golden. Stir in the garlic and cook for 1 minute, then add the vinegar and sugar and cook for a further 3–4 minutes.

- Stir in the beans, raisins, almonds, passata and Worcestershire sauce and season to taste. Simmer for 10–11 minutes until thickened. Stir in the chopped parsley.

- Meanwhile, toast the bread under a preheated hot grill for 2–3 minutes on each side.

- Spoon the beans over the toast and serve sprinkled with the cheese.

10 Boston Baked Beans

Heat 1 tablespoon olive oil in a saucepan, add 1 diced onion and 2 chopped garlic cloves and cook for 3–4 minutes until softened. Stir in 1 teaspoon paprika, 1 tablespoon mango chutney and a 400 g (13 oz) can baked beans and simmer for 2–3 minutes until heated through. Meanwhile, toast 4 slices of wholemeal bread under a preheated hot grill for 2–3 minutes on each side, then spoon over the beans to serve.

30 Spicy Bean Quesadillas

Mix together a rinsed and drained 400 g (13 oz) can black-eyed beans, ½ teaspoon ground cumin, 1 teaspoon dried chilli flakes, 2 sliced spring onions, 1 cored, deseeded and diced red pepper and 75 g (3 oz) grated Cheddar cheese in a bowl, then season. Rub 1 garlic clove over 2 flour tortillas. Spoon the bean mixture over the tortillas and spread to the edges. Top each one with another tortilla. Heat 1 tablespoon olive oil in a frying pan, slide in 1 quesadilla and cook for 3–4 minutes on each side, turning it over gently, until golden and the filling has melted. Remove from the pan and keep warm. Repeat with the remaining quesadilla. Meanwhile, mix together 2 peeled, stoned and diced avocados, the juice of 1 lime and 2 tablespoons chopped coriander in a bowl. Serve the quesadilla cut into wedges, with the avocado salsa on the side.

 # Salmon and Sesame Skewers

Serves 4

1 tablespoon soy sauce

2 teaspoons honey

500g (1 lb) salmon fillet, skinned and cut into strips

4 teaspoons sesame oil

juice of 1 lime

1 cucumber

6 spring onions, finely sliced

16 cherry tomatoes, halved

3 tablespoons sesame seeds

- Mix together the soy sauce and honey in a shallow bowl. Add the salmon and mix well, then cover and leave to marinate in the refrigerator for 12–15 minutes. Meanwhile, soak 8 wooden skewers in water for 10 minutes.

- Mix together the sesame oil and lime juice in a large bowl. Using a vegetable peeler, slice the cucumber into long, thin strips and place in the bowl with the spring onions and cherry tomatoes. Toss in the dressing.

- Thread the salmon on to the skewers, then roll in the sesame seeds to coat. Cook in a preheated hot griddle pan or under a preheated hot grill for 2–3 minutes on each side or until cooked through.

- Serve the salmon skewers with the cucumber salad.

---

1 **Pan-Fried Sesame-Crusted Salmon**

Place 4 tablespoons sesame seeds on a plate. Brush the skin of four 150 g (5 oz) salmon fillets with 1 egg white, then dip into the seeds. Heat 1 tablespoon olive oil in a frying pan, add the salmon, skin side down, and cook for 4–5 minutes, then turn and cook for a further 3 minutes. Meanwhile, mix together 2 tablespoons soy sauce, 1 tablespoon sherry, ½ teaspoon brown sugar, 2 teaspoons peeled and grated fresh root ginger and 1 crushed garlic clove. Pour into the pan and simmer for 2 minutes. Serve the salmon with steamed vegetables and the sauce spooned over.

 2 **Grilled Salmon with Sesame Salad**

Mix together 3 tablespoons soy sauce, 2 teaspoons honey, 1 teaspoon sesame oil, 2 tablespoons olive oil and the juice of ½ lime in a non-metallic bowl. Add 4 salmon fillets, about 150 g (5 oz) each, and leave to marinate for 5 minutes. Meanwhile, dry-fry 2 tablespoons sesame seeds in a nonstick frying pan for 2 minutes, stirring frequently, until golden. Toss together 50 g (2 oz) rocket leaves, 1 chopped cucumber, 100 g (3½ oz) quartered cherry tomatoes, 6 sliced spring onions and the toasted sesame seeds. Cook the salmon under a preheated hot grill for 4–5 minutes on each side or until cooked through. Toss the remaining marinade into the salad and serve with the salmon.

Pancetta and Cannellini Bean Bruschetta

Serves 4

1 small baguette, cut into 8 slices
8 slices of pancetta
1 garlic clove
200 g (7 oz) canned cannellini
  beans, rinsed and drained
2 tablespoons chopped chives
juice of ½ lemon
olive oil, for drizzling
4 cherry tomatoes, halved
pepper

· Toast the bread and pancetta under a preheated hot grill for 2–3 minutes on each side until the bread is toasted and the pancetta crisp. Rub one side of each slice of toast with the garlic clove.

· Meanwhile, place the beans, chives, lemon juice and pepper to taste in a bowl, then mash together very lightly, leaving some of the beans whole.

· Spoon a little of the bean mixture on to the toasts, then drizzle with oil and top each with a crisp pancetta slice and a piece of tomato. Serve immediately.

2 **Pancetta and Cannellini Bean Spaghetti** Cook 400 g (13 oz) spaghetti in a large saucepan of boiling water for 8–9 minutes, or according to the pack instructions, until 'al dente'. Meanwhile, heat 1 tablespoon olive oil in a frying pan, add 2 crushed garlic cloves, 175 g (6 oz) diced pancetta and a pinch of dried chilli flakes and cook for 1 minute. Add a 227 g (7½ oz) can chopped tomatoes and 200 g (7 oz) canned cannellini beans, rinsed and drained, and cook for 2–3 minutes, then stir in 100 g (3½ oz) pitted black olives and 1 tablespoon capers, rinsed and drained. Drain the pasta, then toss into the sauce with 2 tablespoons chopped parsley.

3 **Pancetta-Wrapped Asparagus with Cannellini Bean Salad** Place 100 g (3½ oz) couscous in a heatproof bowl and just cover with boiling water. Leave to stand for 15 minutes, then fluff up with a fork. Meanwhile, finely slice 1 fennel bulb and stir into the couscous with 200 g (7 oz) canned cannellini beans, rinsed and drained, 50 g (2 oz) toasted pine nuts, 50 g (2 oz) sultanas, 2 tablespoons pitted green olives and 1 tablespoon chopped dill. Mix together the juice and grated rind of 1 lemon, 2 tablespoons chopped parsley and 1 chopped garlic clove in a small bowl, then stir into the salad with 1 tablespoon extra virgin olive oil. Season well.

Wrap 12 trimmed asparagus spears in 12 slices of pancetta. Heat 1 tablespoon olive oil in a griddle pan, add the asparagus and cook for 4–5 minutes, turning occasionally, until chargrilled on all sides. Serve with the bean salad.

2 Chickpea and Sprouted Seed Patties

Serves 4

½ red onion, diced

400 g (13 oz) can chickpeas, rinsed and drained

¼ teaspoon cumin seeds

20 g (¾ oz) sun-dried tomatoes

2 tablespoons sprouted seeds, such as mung or lentil

2 tablespoons olive oil

salt and pepper

To serve

mango chutney

crisp green salad

- Place the onion and chickpeas in a food processor or blender and blitz until the chickpeas are broken down. Add all the remaining ingredients except the olive oil, season with salt and pepper and blitz again until the mixture comes together.

- Using wet hands, form the mixture into small patties. Cover and chill for 5 minutes.

- Heat the oil in a large frying pan, add the patties and cook for 4–5 minutes on each side until golden.

- Serve with a little mango chutney and a crisp green salad.

---

1 Chickpea and Alfalfa Salad

Toss together 40 g (1¾ oz) watercress, 1 cored, deseeded and sliced red pepper, 1 cored, deseeded and sliced yellow pepper, 1 sliced small red onion, 100 g (3½ oz) halved cherry tomatoes, a rinsed and drained 400 g (13 oz) can chickpeas and 175 g (6 oz) crumbled feta cheese in a serving bowl. Whisk together the juice of ½ lemon, 3 tablespoons olive oil, 1 deseeded and finely diced chilli, ½ teaspoon Dijon mustard and ½ teaspoon honey in a small bowl, then toss with the salad. Sprinkle with 40 g (1¾ oz) alfalfa sprouts and serve.

3 Chickpea and Sprouted Seed Curry

Heat 2 tablespoons coconut oil in a wok or large saucepan, add 2 chopped onions and 2 garlic cloves and cook over a medium-low heat for 9–10 minutes until starting to caramelize. Increase the heat, add 1 teaspoon ground cumin, ½ teaspoon each of ground coriander, turmeric and chilli powder and a pinch of garam masala and stir-fry for 1–2 minutes, then add 4 chopped tomatoes and cook for 6–8 minutes until the sauce starts to thicken. Add 150 ml (¼ pint) water and mix well, then add 2 rinsed and drained 400 g (13 oz) cans chickpeas and cook for 5 minutes, mashing a few chickpeas while cooking. Stir in a 3.5-cm (1½-inch) piece of fresh root ginger, peeled and grated, 2 tablespoons sprouted seeds and 2 tablespoons chopped coriander. Serve with cooked basmati rice.

Prawn and Courgette Spring Rolls

Serves 4

3 large courgettes
1 large carrot, cut into matchsticks
4 spring onions, shredded
25 g (1 oz) bean sprouts
1 red pepper and 1 yellow pepper,
    cored, deseeded and thinly sliced
100 g (3½ oz) peeled cooked
    prawns
12–15 mint leaves
12–15 coriander leaves

To serve

40 g (1¾ oz) rocket leaves
250 g (8 oz) ready-made salsa

- Using a vegetable peeler, thinly slice the courgettes into long, wide ribbons. Place the slices on a clean surface.

- Place a few pieces of each vegetable, 1 teaspoon of the prawns and a few herbs on to the end of each courgette slice, then roll up to enclose the filling.

- Place the rolls in a steamer and steam for 6–8 minutes until tender.

- Serve with rocket leaves and salsa.

---

20 Vietnamese Prawn Spring Rolls

Mix together 1 diced lemon grass stalk, 2 crushed garlic cloves, 1 teaspoon each of soy sauce and sugar and 2 teaspoons fish sauce. Add 500 g (1 lb) raw peeled prawns, cover and marinate for 6–8 minutes. Heat a wok, and stir-fry the prawns for 5–6 minutes. Set aside. Cut 1 cucumber, 2 carrots and 1 cored and deseeded red pepper into matchsticks. Dip 1 rice paper wrapper into warm water for 2 seconds, then fold in half on a dry surface. Add 1 tablespoon each of the prawns and vegetables and 1 basil and 1 mint leaf, then roll up to enclose the filling. Repeat to make 16. Serve with dipping sauce.

30 Prawn, Chicken and Vegetable

Spring Rolls Heat 1 tablespoon groundnut oil in a wok or frying pan, add 200 g (7 oz) diced chicken breast and 50 g (2 oz) chopped chestnut mushrooms and cook for 2–3 minutes. Stir in 1 tablespoon soy sauce and 1 teaspoon Chinese five-spice powder. Remove from the heat and add 100 g (3½ oz) cooked peeled prawns, 1 teaspoon peeled and grated fresh root ginger, 75 g (3 oz) bean sprouts, 2 diced spring onions, 1 grated courgette and 1 small carrot, peeled and cut into matchsticks. Lay 2 spring roll wrappers on top of each other and spoon 2 tablespoons of the filling into the centre. Brush the corners of the wrapper with beaten egg and fold in the edges, then roll up to enclose the filling. Repeat with the remaining ingredients to make 12. Place on a large baking sheet and brush with 25 g (1 oz) melted butter. Bake in a preheated oven, 200°C (400°F), Gas Mark 6, for 10–12 minutes until golden and heated through. Serve immediately with sweet chilli dipping sauce.

QuickCook

Meat and Poultry

Recipes listed by cooking time

30

20

Chicken Dippers with Homemade Hummus

Serves 4

1 tablespoon plain flour
1 tablespoon chopped parsley
1 tablespoon chopped coriander
300 g (10 oz) chicken mini-fillets
25 g (1 oz) butter
1 tablespoon olive oil

For the hummus

1 garlic clove, finely diced
400 g (13 oz) can chickpeas,
  rinsed and drained
juice of ½ lemon
2 tablespoons tahini paste
3–4 tablespoons extra virgin
  olive oil

- Mix together the flour and herbs on a plate, then toss the chicken strips in the herbed flour.

- Heat the butter and olive oil in a large frying pan, add the chicken and cook for 3–4 minutes on each side or until golden and cooked through.

- Meanwhile, make the hummus. Place the garlic, chickpeas, lemon juice and tahini in a food processor or blender and blend until nearly smooth. With the motor still running, pour in the extra virgin olive oil through the feed tube and blend to the desired consistency.

- Serve the chicken with hummus for dipping.

2 **Spiced Chicken Breasts with Hummus** Mix together 1 crushed garlic clove and ½ tablespoon each of paprika, dried thyme, cayenne pepper and ground black pepper in a small bowl, then rub over 4 boneless, skinless chicken breasts, about 150 g (5 oz) each. Cook the chicken breasts under a preheated hot grill for 6–8 minutes on each side or until cooked through. Spoon a 300 g (10 oz) tub of ready-made hummus into a bowl. Serve the chicken with the hummus and a rocket salad.

3 **Spicy Pancetta-Wrapped Chicken with Aubergine Dip** Place 4 boneless, skinless chicken breasts, about 150 g (5 oz) each, between 2 sheets of clingfilm and bash with a meat mallet or rolling pin until about 5 mm (¼ inch) thick. Lay each one on 2 slices of pancetta, spread each with 1 tablespoon harissa paste and 50 g (2 oz) chopped mozzarella cheese and roll up. Place on a baking sheet, drizzle with a little olive oil and cook in a preheated oven, 200°C (400°F), Gas Mark 6, for 20–25 minutes or until cooked through. Meanwhile, prick 1 kg (2 lb) large aubergines all over with a fork and cook over an open gas (or barbecue) flame, turning frequently, for 15–20 minutes until blackened and cooked through. Peel off and discard the skin while warm, then put the flesh into a bowl. Mash with a fork, then add 125 g (4 oz) tahini paste and the juice of 2–3 lemons and season to taste. Slice the chicken and serve with the aubergine dip and steamed green beans.

Lamb Koftas with Mint Yogurt

Serves 4

400 g (13 oz) minced lamb
1 teaspoon ground cumin
1 teaspoon ground coriander
1 teaspoon turmeric
3 tablespoons chopped coriander
1 red chilli, deseeded and diced
4 garlic cloves, crushed
1 small egg, beaten
1 tablespoon olive oil
salt and pepper
salad leaves, to serve

For the mint yogurt

250 g (8 oz) Greek yogurt
1 tablespoon chopped mint
½ cucumber, grated
juice of ½ lemon

- Place the lamb, spices, fresh coriander, chilli, garlic, salt and pepper and egg into a food processor and blitz together. Using wet hands, roll the mixture into walnut-sized balls, then shape the balls around 8 metal skewers.

- Heat the oil in an ovenproof frying pan, add the skewers and cook for 2–3 minutes on all sides, then transfer to a preheated oven, 220°C (425°F), Gas Mark 7, for a further 6–8 minutes until cooked through.

- Meanwhile, to make the mint yogurt, mix together all the ingredients in a bowl.

- Serve the koftas with a few salad leaves and the mint yogurt.

---

1 Lamb Chops with Cucumber and Mint Salad Cook 8 lamb cutlets under a preheated hot grill for 3–4 minutes on each side, or until cooked to your liking. Meanwhile, using a vegetable peeler, slice 2 cucumbers into long, thin strips. Place in a serving bowl and mix together with 2 tablespoons shredded mint, the seeds of 1 pomegranate and 40 g (1¾ oz) watercress. Whisk together 3 tablespoons olive oil, 1 tablespoon sherry vinegar, ½ teaspoon mustard and ½ teaspoon honey in a bowl, then toss with the salad. Serve with the lamb.

3 Mint-Crusted Rack of Lamb Heat 50 g (2 oz) butter and 1 tablespoon olive oil in an ovenproof frying pan, add 2 racks of French-trimmed lamb and cook for 2–3 minutes on each side to brown. Cover the bones with foil, then transfer to a preheated oven, 170°C (340°F), Gas Mark 3, and cook for a further 4–5 minutes. Leave to rest for 5 minutes. Meanwhile, place 3 tablespoons chopped mint, 2 crushed garlic cloves and 75 g (3 oz) fresh wholemeal breadcrumbs in a food processor and whizz to a paste. Brush the lamb with 2 tablespoons Dijon mustard and press on the paste. Return to the oven for 5–10 minutes, or until cooked to your liking. Leave to rest for 3 minutes. Serve with steamed broccoli.

Chicken Pasta Salad with Pesto Dressing

Serves 4

2 boneless, skinless chicken breasts
½ tablespoon olive oil
150 g (5 oz) conchiglie pasta
4 tablespoons walnut halves
1 small red onion, sliced
225 g (7½ oz) baby plum tomatoes, halved
½ cucumber, cut into chunks
100 g (3½ oz) watercress
2 tablespoons Parmesan cheese shavings, to serve

For the dressing

1½ tablespoons olive oil
2 tablespoons ready-made pesto
1 tablespoon balsamic vinegar

- To make the pesto dressing, whisk together all the ingredients in a small bowl and set aside.

- Brush the chicken breasts with the oil, then cook in a preheated hot griddle pan for 12–15 minutes, turning once, until cooked through.

- Meanwhile, cook the pasta in a saucepan of boiling water for 8–9 minutes, or according to the pack instructions, until 'al dente'. Drain, then refresh under cold running water and drain again.

- Heat a nonstick frying pan over a medium-low heat and dry-fry the walnuts for 3–4 minutes, stirring frequently, until slightly golden.

- Thinly slice the chicken, then place in a large bowl with the pasta, toasted walnuts, onion, tomatoes, cucumber and watercress.

- Toss with the pesto dressing and serve sprinkled with the Parmesan cheese shavings.

---

1 **Chicken Pesto Baguettes**

Halve 4 baguettes horizontally and spread the bases of each with ½ tablespoon ready-made pesto. Divide 50 g (2 oz) watercress between the baguettes and top with 4 sliced tomatoes, ¼ sliced cucumber, ½ sliced red onion and 2 sliced shop-bought ready-cooked chicken breasts. Top each with a dollop of mayonnaise, then replace the tops.

3 **Roasted Chicken Breasts with Pesto Pasta** Rub 4 boneless, skinless chicken breasts with olive oil and season, then cook in a preheated hot ovenproof griddle pan for 2–3 minutes on each side. Transfer to a preheated oven, 200°C (400°F), Gas Mark 6, for 16–18 minutes or until cooked through. Meanwhile, cook 350 g (11½ oz) linguine in a saucepan of boiling water for 8–9 minutes, or according to the pack instructions, until 'al dente'. Drain, then return to the pan and toss together with 4 tablespoons ready-made pesto, 50 g (2 oz) chopped watercress and 75 g (3 oz) halved tomatoes. Serve topped with the roasted chicken breasts and 2 tablespoons grated Pecorino cheese.

30 Chicken and Apricot Stew

Serves 4

1 tablespoon olive oil
2 garlic cloves, crushed
1 tablespoon peeled and grated
  fresh root ginger
1 large onion, chopped
600 g (1¼ lb) chicken breast
  fillets, cubed
100 g (3½ oz) red split lentils
1 teaspoon ground cumin
¼ teaspoon ground cinnamon
¼ teaspoon turmeric
¼ teaspoon ground coriander
12 ready-to-eat dried apricots
juice of 1 lemon
750 ml (1¼ pints) hot chicken stock
1 tablespoon chopped mint
1 tablespoon chopped coriander
seeds of 1 pomegranate
2 tablespoons toasted flaked
  almonds
couscous, to serve

- Heat the oil in a large saucepan, add the garlic, ginger and onion and cook for 1–2 minutes. Add the chicken and cook for a further 5 minutes, stirring occasionally.

- Stir in the lentils, spices, apricots and lemon juice and stir well. Pour in the stock and bring to the boil, then reduce the heat and simmer for 15 minutes.

- Stir in the herbs and pomegranate seeds, then sprinkle with the almonds. Serve in bowls with couscous.

---

1 Chicken and Apricot Wraps

Spread 4 tortilla wraps with 2 tablespoons mayonnaise. Top each with the leaves of ½ Little Gem lettuce, ½ cored, deseeded and sliced red pepper, 2 chopped ready-to-eat dried apricots, a few coriander leaves, 100 g (3½ oz) shop-bought ready-cooked chicken breasts, diced, and 2 teaspoons mango chutney. Roll up the wraps and serve.

2 Chicken and Apricot Kebabs

Mix together 2 tablespoons olive oil, the juice and grated rind of 1 orange and 1 teaspoon each of ground cumin and dried chilli flakes in a large non-metallic bowl. Add 500 g (1 lb) cubed chicken breast fillets, 12 ready-to-eat dried apricots and 2 cored, deseeded and chopped red peppers and mix well to coat. Leave to marinate for 3–4 minutes. Thread the chicken, apricots and pepper on to 8 metal skewers, then cook under a preheated hot grill or on a barbecue for 10–12 minutes, turning occasionally, until the chicken is cooked through. Sprinkle with chopped coriander and serve with cooked brown rice or quinoa.

Beef and Lentil Chilli

Serves 4

1 tablespoon olive oil
1 large onion, diced
2 garlic cloves, crushed
1 red pepper, cored, deseeded
  and diced
1 teaspoon chilli powder
1 teaspoon paprika
1 teaspoon ground cumin
250 g (8 oz) minced beef
400 g (13 oz) can green lentils,
  rinsed and drained
200 ml (7 fl oz) water
400 g (13 oz) can tomatoes
½ teaspoon sugar
2 tablespoons tomato purée
400 g (13 oz) can kidney beans,
  rinsed and drained
cooked long grain rice, to serve

- Heat the oil in a saucepan, add the onion and cook for 1 minute. Add the garlic and red pepper and cook for 1 minute, then stir in the spices. Add the beef and cook, stirring occasionally, for a further 4 minutes until browned.

- Stir in the lentils, measurement water, tomatoes, sugar and tomato purée into the mixture. Bring to a simmer and cook for 10–12 minutes, breaking the tomatoes up with a wooden spoon. Stir in the kidney beans and cook for 2 minutes until heated through.

- Serve the chilli with cooked rice.

---

10 **Quick Beef and Lentil Spaghetti Bolognese** Cook 400 g (13 oz) spaghetti in a saucepan of boiling water for 8–9 minutes, or according to the pack instructions. Meanwhile, heat 1 tablespoon olive oil in a saucepan, add 250 g (8 oz) minced beef and cook until browned. Stir in a rinsed and drained 400 g (13 oz) can green lentils and 300 g (10 oz) ready-made Bolognese sauce. Simmer for 8 minutes. Drain the spaghetti and stir into the sauce. Serve sprinkled with Parmesan cheese shavings.

30 **Beef and Lentil Cottage Pie** Heat 1 tablespoon olive oil in a large frying pan, add 1 chopped onion, 1 crushed garlic clove, 2 diced celery sticks and 2 peeled and diced carrots and cook for 1–2 minutes. Add 250 g (8 oz) minced beef and cook for 5 minutes. Stir in a rinsed and drained 400 g (13 oz) can green lentils, a 400 g (13 oz) can chopped tomatoes, 300 ml (½ pint) beef stock, 1 teaspoon dried mixed herbs and a dash of Worcestershire sauce. Season and simmer for 15 minutes.

Meanwhile, cook 875 g (1¾ lb) peeled and chopped potatoes in a saucepan of boiling water for 10–12 minutes until tender. Drain and mash in the pan with 25 g (1 oz) butter, 2 tablespoons milk and 2 teaspoons wholegrain mustard. Spoon the beef mixture into an ovenproof dish and top with the mash. Cook in a preheated oven, 200°C (400°F), Gas Mark 6, for 10 minutes until golden.

30 Chicken and Tarragon Risotto

Serves 4

2 tablespoons olive oil

4 boneless, skinless chicken breasts, about 150 g (5 oz) each, seasoned

50 g (2 oz) butter

1 onion, finely chopped

2 garlic cloves, crushed

375 g (12 oz) Arborio risotto rice

splash of white wine

1 litre (1¾ pints) hot chicken stock

200 g (7 oz) asparagus tips

1 tablespoon chopped tarragon

4 tablespoons grated Parmesan cheese

salt and pepper

- Heat half the oil in a heatproof frying pan, add the chicken and cook for 4–5 minutes on each side until browned. Transfer to a preheated oven, 200°C (400°F), Gas Mark 6, and cook for a further 15–18 minutes or until cooked through.

- Meanwhile, heat the remaining oil and butter in a pan, add the onion and garlic and cook for 2–3 minutes. Stir in the rice, then add the wine and simmer until absorbed. Add a ladle of stock and cook, stirring, until absorbed. Continue adding more stock until the rice is cooked 'al dente', about 18–20 minutes.

- While the risotto is cooking, steam the asparagus for 3–4 minutes until tender, then cut in half. Stir the asparagus, tarragon and half the cheese into the risotto, then season.

- Slice the chicken breasts diagonally. Serve the risotto topped with the chicken and sprinkled with the remaining Parmesan.

---

10 Chicken and Tarragon Double-Decker Sandwiches Mix together 1 tablespoon chopped tarragon and 2 tablespoons mayonnaise. Toast 12 slices of wholemeal bread under a preheated hot grill for 2–3 minutes on each side, then spread 4 slices with the mayonnaise. Divide 4 sliced tomatoes and 2–3 leaves of iceburg lettuce between the slices, then top each with another slice of toast. Spread each of these with 2 teaspoons mango chutney, then add slices of ready-cooked chicken and cucumber. Top with the remaining toast and cut each into 4 triangles to serve.

20 Chicken and Tarragon Tagliatelle Heat 1 tablespoon olive oil in a frying pan, add 300 g (10 oz) chopped chicken breast fillets and cook for 5–6 minutes. Pour in 2 tablespoons white wine and simmer for 4–5 minutes until the liquid has reduced. Stir in 2 chopped garlic cloves, 200 ml (7 fl oz) natural yogurt and 3 tablespoons roughly chopped tarragon and simmer for 5–6 minutes or until the chicken is cooked through. Meanwhile, cook 400 g (13 oz) tagliatelle in a saucepan of boiling water for 8–10 minutes, or according to the pack instructions, until 'al dente'. Drain, then toss in the pan with 100 g (3½ oz) baby spinach leaves until the leaves are wilted. Mix in the chicken, season well and serve sprinkled with Parmesan cheese shavings.

20 Pork, Apple and Ginger Stir-Fry

Serves 4

2 tablespoons sesame seeds
1 tablespoon coconut oil
300 g (10 oz) pork fillet, in strips
2 garlic cloves, chopped
5-cm (2-inch) fresh root ginger,
 peeled and cut into matchsticks
1 green chilli, deseeded and
 chopped
2 apples, cored and cut into
 wedges
2 carrots, cut into matchsticks
150 g (5 oz) broccoli florets
300 g (10 oz) ribbon rice noodles
juice of 1 lime

- Heat a nonstick frying pan over a medium-low heat and dry-fry the sesame seeds for 2 minutes, stirring frequently, until golden and toasted. Set aside.

- Heat the oil in a wok or large frying pan, add the pork and stir-fry for 6–8 minutes until lightly browned. Add the garlic, ginger, chilli, apples and vegetables and stir-fry for a further 4–5 minutes or until the pork is cooked through.

- Meanwhile, cook the noodles according to the pack instructions, then add to the stir-fry with the lime juice and toss all the ingredients together.

- Serve sprinkled with the toasted sesame seeds.

---

10 Grilled Pork Steaks with Apple and Ginger Coleslaw

Cook 4 pork steaks, about 150 g (5 oz) each, under a preheated hot grill for 3–4 minutes on each side or until cooked through. Meanwhile, finely slice 1 small white cabbage, 2 celery sticks and 1 cored and deseeded red pepper and place in a bowl. Add 2 peeled and grated carrots and 2 peeled, cored and grated apples and mix well. Mix together 2 tablespoons natural yogurt, a 2.5-cm (1-inch) piece of fresh root ginger, peeled and grated, 1 tablespoon mayonnaise in a small bowl, then stir into the coleslaw with 2 tablespoons chopped coriander. Serve with the grilled pork.

30 Apple and Ginger Pork

Toss 500 g (1 lb) chopped pork loin in seasoned flour. Heat 1 tablespoon olive oil in a large frying pan, add the pork and cook for 4–6 minutes until browned. Remove with a slotted spoon and set aside. Add 2 peeled, cored and sliced apples to the pan and cook for 3 minutes until slightly browned. Stir in 2 chopped garlic cloves, 1 tablespoon peeled and chopped fresh root ginger and 1 teaspoon each of ground coriander, ground cumin and mustard seeds and cook, stirring, for a further 2–3 minutes. Pour in 200 ml (7 fl oz) hot chicken stock and add the reserved pork. Bring to a simmer and cook for 10 minutes until the pork is cooked through and the sauce has started to thicken. Serve with cooked basmati rice and sprinkle with chopped coriander.

20 Lamb Cutlets with Pea and Rosemary Mash

Serves 4

750 g (1 lb 10 oz) potatoes,
peeled and chopped
350 g (11½ oz) frozen or
fresh peas
1 tablespoon chopped rosemary
8 lamb cutlets
30 g (1 oz) butter
salt and pepper

- Cook the potatoes in a pan of boiling water for 12–15 minutes until tender, adding the peas 2 minutes before the end of the cooking time.

- Meanwhile, sprinkle half the rosemary over the lamb cutlets then cook them under a preheated hot grill for 3–4 minutes on each side, or until cooked to your liking. Leave to rest.

- Drain the potatoes and peas, then return to the pan and lightly mash with the remaining rosemary, butter and salt and pepper to taste. Serve the lamb cutlets accompanied by the pea and rosemary mash.

---

10 Rosemary Lamb Cutlets with Summer Salad Mix together 2 tablespoons chopped rosemary and 1 tablespoon olive oil in a small bowl, then rub over 8 lamb cutlets. Cook under a preheated hot grill for 3–4 minutes on each side, or until cooked to your liking. Meanwhile, cook 100 g (3½ oz) fresh or frozen peas, 75 g (3 oz) broad beans and 125 g (4 oz) asparagus tips in a saucepan of boiling water for 2–3 minutes. Drain, refresh under cold running water and drain again, then toss together with 2 carrots, peeled and cut into matchsticks, 12 baby sweetcorn, the torn leaves of 1 romaine lettuce, a small handful of mint leaves and 12 cherry tomatoes in a serving bowl. Drizzle with 2 tablespoons extra virgin olive oil and the juice of 1 lemon. Serve with the lamb.

30 Lamb Racks with Rosemary and Garlic Cut small slits into 4 x 3-cutlet racks of lamb and insert 2 sliced garlic cloves and 4 rosemary sprigs into the slits. Whisk together 1 tablespoon honey, 2 tablespoons wholegrain mustard and 1 tablespoon ready-made mint sauce in a bowl, then brush over the lamb. Leave to marinate for 10 minutes. Place in a roasting tin and cook in a preheated oven, 200°C (400°F), Gas Mark 6, for 18 minutes, or until cooked to your liking, basting with the marinade 2 or 3 times. Serve the lamb with griddled asparagus and mashed potatoes.

HEA-MEAT-VEZ

30 Chicken with Orange and Olives

Serves 4

2 tablespoons olive oil
4 boneless, skinless chicken
  breasts, about 150 g (5 oz) each
750 ml (1¼ pints) chicken stock
a few thyme sprigs
12 black olives, pitted
2 oranges, segmented
225 g (7½ oz) bulgar wheat
3 tablespoons toasted flaked
  almonds
2 tablespoons chopped parsley
salt and pepper

· Heat the oil in a large frying pan, add the chicken and cook for 3–4 minutes on each side until browned. Pour in 450 ml (¾ pint) of the stock, then stir in the thyme, olives and orange segments. Cover and simmer for 15–16 minutes until cooked through.

· Meanwhile, place the bulgar wheat in a saucepan with the remaining stock, season to taste and simmer for 8–10 minutes until most of the water is absorbed. Remove the pan from the heat and stir in the almonds, then cover and leave to stand.

· Remove the chicken from the frying pan and keep warm. Simmer the sauce for 4–5 minutes until reduced by half. Stir in the chopped parsley.

· Serve the chicken with the bulgar wheat, drizzled with the thyme, olive and orange sauce.

---

1 Chicken, Orange and Olive Sandwiches Toast 8 slices of wholemeal bread under a preheated hot grill for 2–3 minutes on each side. Spread 4 of the slices with 2 teaspoons ready-made pesto each, then top each with a small handful of bistro salad leaves, a few orange segments, 2–3 slices of shop-bought ready-cooked chicken, 1 sliced tomato and 2–3 sliced pitted olives. Top with the remaining toast and serve.

2 Grilled Chicken, Orange and Olive Salad Mix together 2 crushed garlic cloves, 2 tablespoons olive oil and 2 tablespoons chopped basil in a dish, then add 4 boneless, skinless chicken breasts, about 150 g (5 oz) each, and leave to marinate for 2–3 minutes. Heat a griddle pan until hot, add the chicken breasts and cook for 6–8 minutes on each side or until cooked through. Meanwhile, toss together 1 roughly torn romaine lettuce, 25 g (1 oz) rocket leaves, 1 sliced red onion, 12 pitted black olives and 100 g (3½ oz) halved cherry tomatoes in a serving bowl. Segment 2 oranges over a bowl to catch the juice, then add the segments to the salad. Whisk together the reserved juice, 3 tablespoons olive oil and ½ teaspoon each of caster sugar and mustard. Cut the chicken into thick slices and add to the salad. Serve sprinkled with the dressing.

Harissa Beef Fajitas

Serves 4

3 teaspoons harissa paste
½ teaspoon paprika
2 tablespoons olive oil
525 g (1 lb 2 oz) rump steak,
  cut into thick strips
8 tortilla wraps
½ iceburg lettuce, shredded
4 tablespoons soured cream
4 tablespoons ready-made
  guacamole
4 tablespoons ready-made
  tomato salsa
4 tablespoons grated Cheddar
  cheese

- Mix together the harissa, paprika and oil in a non-metallic bowl. Add the steak and mix to coat, then cover and leave to marinate for 5 minutes.

- Heat a griddle pan until hot, add the steak and cook for 20 seconds on each side, or until cooked to your liking. Remove from the pan and keep warm.

- Heat the tortillas in a microwave according to the pack instructions. Sprinkle some shredded lettuce in the centre of each tortilla and layer the steak on top. Spoon a little soured cream, guacamole and salsa over the steak, then sprinkle over the cheese. Roll up the wraps and serve.

Harissa Beef Salad

Mix together 3 teaspoons harissa paste and 2 tablespoons olive oil in a bowl, then rub over 3 rump steaks, about 150 g (5 oz) each. Cover and leave to marinate for 10 minutes. Meanwhile, toss together 1 chopped cucumber, 4 chopped tomatoes, 4 spring onions, ½ thickly shredded iceburg lettuce, a handful of mint leaves and a handful of coriander leaves in a bowl. Whisk together 2 teaspoons caster sugar, 2 tablespoons fish sauce, the juice of 1 lime and 2 tablespoons olive oil, then pour over the salad. Heat a griddle pan until hot, add the steaks and cook for 2–3 minutes on each side, or until cooked to your liking. Leave to rest for 2–3 minutes. Slice the steak across the grain and add to the salad. Serve sprinkled with 2 tablespoons chopped peanuts.

Harissa Beef Burgers

Place 525 g (1 lb 2 oz) minced beef, 2 tablespoons chopped coriander, 1 tablespoon harissa paste, 1 chopped onion, 1 egg yolk, 1 tablespoon olive oil and salt and pepper in a food processor and blend together. Shape into 4 equal-sized burgers, cover and chill for 10 minutes. Cook the burgers under a preheated medium grill for 15 minutes, turning once. Toast 4 halved burger buns. Place a burger on each base and top with iceburg lettuce, sliced tomatoes, sliced red onion and a dollop of mayonnaise or soured cream. Top with the lids and serve.

Ginger Chicken Soup

Serves 4

1 tablespoon groundnut oil

2.5-cm (1-inch) piece of fresh
  root ginger, peeled and grated

300 g (10 oz) chicken breast
  fillets, cut into strips

1 litre (1¾ pints) hot chicken stock

4 pak choi, sliced

175 g (6 oz) dried egg noodles

2 tablespoons sesame seeds

- Heat the oil in a wok or large saucepan, add the ginger and stir-fry for 1 minute, then stir in the chicken and 125 ml (4 fl oz) of the stock. Bring to the boil, then cook over a high heat for 5 minutes or until the chicken is cooked through.

- Add the remaining stock and bring to a simmer. Stir in the pak choi and noodles and simmer for 5 minutes until the noodles are cooked.

- Meanwhile, heat a nonstick frying pan over a medium-low heat and dry-fry the sesame seeds for 2 minutes, stirring frequently, until golden brown and toasted.

- Ladle the soup into bowls and serve sprinkled with the toasted sesame seeds.

---

1  **Ginger Chicken Wraps**

Heat 1 tablespoon olive oil in a frying pan, add 450 g (14½ oz) thinly sliced chicken breast fillets, 1 tablespoon peeled and grated fresh root ginger, 2 diced garlic cloves and 6 sliced spring onions and fry, stirring, for 5–6 minutes or until the chicken is cooked through. Divide the chicken between 4 tortilla wraps, then top with 1 red and 1 yellow pepper, both cored, deseeded and sliced, and ½ shredded romaine lettuce. Roll up the wraps and serve.

3 **Ginger Chicken Stir-Fry**

Heat 1 tablespoon olive oil or coconut oil in a wok, add 2 crushed garlic cloves, a 5-cm (2-inch) piece of fresh root ginger, peeled and grated, and 450 g (14½ oz) sliced chicken breast fillets and stir-fry for 3–4 minutes. Add 4 chopped spring onions, 2 peeled and sliced carrots and 50 g (2 oz) halved baby sweetcorn and stir-fry for a further 4–5 minutes. Add 2 tablespoons soy sauce, 2 tablespoons oyster sauce and 100 ml (3½ fl oz) water

and simmer for 15 minutes. Stir in 2 chopped pak choi and 50 g (2 oz) bean sprouts and cook for 2–3 minutes until heated through. Serve with cooked basmati rice.

3 Bacon and Leek Tortilla

Serves 4-6

4 tablespoons olive oil
2 leeks, trimmed and thickly sliced
350 g (11½ oz) new potatoes, sliced
4 back bacon rashers, chopped
6 large eggs
75 g (3 oz) mature Cheddar cheese, grated
salt and pepper

- Heat the oil in a large flameproof frying pan, add the leeks and potatoes and sauté for 8–10 minutes, stirring frequently, until golden and tender. Add the bacon and fry for a further 4–5 minutes.

- Meanwhile, beat the eggs in a large bowl and add the cheese. Season well.

- Stir the potato mixture into the beaten eggs, then return to the pan and cook over a low heat for 8–10 minutes, making sure the bottom does not over-cook.

- Place the pan under a preheated hot grill and cook for a further 3–4 minutes until the tortilla is cooked through and golden.

- Serve cut into wedges.

1 Leek, Butternut and Bacon Soup

Heat 2 tablespoons olive oil in a saucepan, add 3 trimmed and diced leeks and 400 g (13 oz) peeled, deseeded and diced butternut squash and cook for 3 minutes. Pour in 900 ml (1½ pints) hot vegetable stock and bring to the boil, then reduce the heat and simmer for 4–5 minutes until the vegetables are soft. Meanwhile, cook 4 back bacon rashers under a preheated hot grill until crisp, then roughly chop. Stir 300 ml (½ pint) soya milk into the soup, then, using a hand-hand blender, blend the soup until smooth. Season to taste. Serve sprinkled with the bacon.

2 Bacon and Leek Penne

Cook 350 g (11½ oz) penne in a saucepan of boiling water for 10–12 minutes until 'al dente'. Meanwhile, heat 2 tablespoons olive oil in a frying pan, add 100 g (3½ oz) bacon lardons and cook for 2–3 minutes. Add 2 trimmed and sliced leeks and 2 crushed garlic cloves and cook for a further 6–8 minutes, then stir in 2 chopped tomatoes and 2 tablespoons chopped parsley. Drain the pasta and toss in the pan with the bacon mixture. Season and serve sprinkled with grated Parmesan cheese.

HEA-MEAT-SOE

30 Spicy Chicken with Cucumber and Radish Salad

Serves 4

4 tablespoons honey
2 tablespoons soy sauce
juice of ½ lemon
a few drops of Tabasco
2 garlic cloves, crushed
4 chicken breasts, about 150 g
  (5 oz) each
2 tablespoons sesame seeds,
  toasted

For the salad

1 cucumber
1 tablespoon sea salt
2 tablespoons caster sugar
1 tablespoon boiling water
4 tablespoons white wine vinegar
1 teaspoon freshly ground
  black pepper
a handful of dill, finely chopped
6 radishes, thinly sliced

- Mix together the honey, soy sauce, lemon juice, Tabasco and garlic in a non-metallic bowl, then brush over the chicken breasts. Cover and leave to marinate in the refrigerator for 10 minutes. Cook under a preheated hot grill for 6–8 minutes on each side, brushing frequently with the marinade, until cooked through.

- Meanwhile, make the salad. Using a vegetable peeler or mandolin, thinly slice the cucumber. Place in a colander and toss with the salt. Leave to stand for 10 minutes to allow the juices to run out.

- Place the sugar and water in a bowl and stir until the sugar is dissolved. Add the vinegar, pepper and dill. Chill for 2 minutes.

- Wrap the cucumber in a clean tea towel and squeeze gently to remove any excess water, then stir into the dill mixture with the radishes. Cover and chill until ready to serve.

- Divide the salad between 4 plates. Slice the chicken breasts and add to the salad. Serve sprinkled with the sesame seeds.

---

10 Spicy Chicken, Cucumber and Radish Pittas Toast 4 wholemeal pitta breads under a preheated grill, until warmed through, then cut down 1 long edge to form pockets. Meanwhile, mix together ½ sliced cucumber, 6 sliced radishes, 1 tablespoon chopped dill and 50 g (2 oz) baby spinach leaves in a bowl, then gently toss with 300 g (10 oz) shop-bought chicken tikka slices and 3–4 tablespoons Caesar salad dressing. Stuff into the pittas and serve.

20 Spicy Chicken with Cucumber and Radish Stir-Fry Mix together 2 tablespoons honey, the juice of 2 limes, 2 tablespoons Chinese five-spice powder and 1 teaspoon sesame oil in a bowl, then spread over 8 chicken drumsticks. Place in an ovenproof dish and bake in a preheated oven, 200°C (400°F), Gas Mark 6, for 16–18 minutes or until cooked through. Meanwhile, mix together 4 chopped pak choi,

1 peeled and thinly sliced carrot, 40 g (1¾ oz) bean sprouts, ¼ deseeded and sliced cucumber, 6 sliced radishes, 2 tablespoons soy sauce, a 2.5-cm (1-inch) piece of peeled and chopped fresh root ginger and a pinch of dried chilli flakes in a bowl. Heat 1 tablespoon groundnut oil in a wok, add the vegetables and stir-fry for 5–6 minutes until starting to wilt. Serve hot with the crispy chicken.

 # Horseradish Beef with Quinoa

Serves 4

625 g (1¼ lb) beef fillet, rolled
  and tied
1 tablespoon creamed horseradish
2 tablespoons olive oil
300 g (10 oz) quinoa
1 red onion, thinly sliced
125 g (4 oz) chestnut mushrooms,
  sliced
1 tablespoon chopped parsley
1 tablespoon chopped mint
40 g (1¾ oz) rocket leaves
3 tablespoons balsamic glaze

- Brush the beef with the horseradish. Heat 1 tablespoon of the oil in a frying pan over a high heat, add the beef and sear on all sides until browned. Transfer to a roasting tin and place in a preheated oven, 200°C (400° F), Gas Mark 6, for 20 minutes. Cover with foil and leave to rest for 5–6 minutes, then slice.

- Meanwhile, cook the quinoa in a saucepan of boiling water for 8–9 minutes, or according to the pack instructions.

- Heat the remaining oil in a large frying pan, add the onion and cook for 2 minutes, then add the mushrooms and cook for a further 5–6 minutes until softened. Remove from the heat and stir in the chopped herbs.

- Drain the quinoa and stir into the mushroom mixture. Divide between 4 warm plates and top with the rocket and sliced beef. Serve drizzled with the balsamic glaze.

---

1 Horseradish Steak Sandwiches

Drizzle 1 tablespoon olive oil over four 175 g (6 oz) rump steaks and season. Heat a griddle pan to hot and cook the steaks for 3 minutes on each side, or to your liking, then leave to rest. Reduce the heat to medium and cook 1 onion, sliced into rings, for 1 minute on each side. Meanwhile, toast 4 split ciabatta rolls under a preheated hot grill. Mix 4 tablespoons mayo with 2 teaspoons creamed horseradish, then spread over the bases. Top with the torn leaves of ½ romaine lettuce, the onion, the sliced steak and 4 sliced tomatoes. Top with the lids and serve.

2 Steak and Chickpea Salad with Horseradish Dressing

Toss together 2 rinsed and drained 400 g (13 oz) cans chickpeas, 1 sliced red onion, 200 g (7 oz) halved cherry tomatoes and a small handful of chopped parsley in a serving bowl. Season 400 g (13 oz) sirloin steak. Heat a griddle pan until piping hot, add the steak and cook for 3 minutes on each side, or until cooked to your liking, then leave to rest. Whisk together 250 ml (8 fl oz) natural yogurt, 1 tablespoon creamed horseradish, 1 tablespoon olive oil and the juice of ½ lemon in a bowl. Slice the steak, toss with the chickpeas and drizzle with the yogurt dressing.

 # Chicken and Vegetable Stir-Fry

Serves 4

2 tablespoons coconut oil

3-cm (1¼-inch) piece of fresh root ginger, peeled and finely diced

2 garlic cloves, crushed

1 onion, chopped

450 g (14½ oz) chicken breast fillets, cut into strips

125 g (4 oz) mushrooms, quartered

300 g (10 oz) broccoli florets

125 g (4 oz) curly kale, chopped

1–2 tablespoons soy sauce

2 tablespoons sesame seeds

- Heat the oil in a wok or large frying pan until hot, add the ginger, garlic and onion and stir-fry for 30 seconds. Add the chicken and stir-fry for a further 2–3 minutes.

- Add the vegetables, then sprinkle over the soy sauce. Stir-fry for 1–2 minutes, then cover and steam for a further 4–5 minutes until the vegetables are tender and the chicken is cooked through.

- Serve sprinkled with the sesame seeds.

2 Chicken and Oriental Vegetable Stir-Fry

Heat 2 tablespoons coconut oil in a wok until hot, add 6 chopped spring onions, 2 crushed garlic cloves and 1 tablespoon peeled and grated root ginger and stir-fry for 2 minutes. Add 450 g (14½ oz) chicken breast fillets in strips, and stir-fry for 2–3 minutes. Add 75 g (3 oz) baby sweetcorn and 1 cored, deseeded and sliced red pepper and stir-fry for a further 3–4 minutes. Stir in 100 g (3½ oz) chopped shiitake mushrooms, 50 g (2 oz) bean sprouts and 2 chopped pak choi and stir-fry for 4–5 minutes. Stir in 2 tablespoons oyster sauce and 1 teaspoon soy sauce and cook for a further 4–5 minutes. Serve sprinkled with 2 tablespoons toasted sesame seeds.

3 Chicken, Vegetable and Noodle Stir-Fry

Mix together 3 tablespoons soy sauce, 2 tablespoons red wine, 2 crushed garlic cloves, 2 teaspoons honey and 1 teaspoon Dijon mustard in a non-metallic bowl. Add 500 g (1 lb) chicken breast fillets, cut into thick strips, and toss in the marinade. Leave to marinate for about 15 minutes. Drain, reserving the marinade. Heat 2 teaspoons groundnut oil in a wok or large frying pan until hot, add half the drained chicken and stir-fry for 2–3 minutes or until cooked through, then remove with a slotted spoon and keep warm. Repeat with the remaining chicken. Add 2 thinly sliced garlic cloves, a 3.5-cm (1½-inch) piece of fresh root ginger, peeled and cut into strips, and 2 carrots, peeled and cut into batons, to the pan and stir-fry for 3–4 minutes. Add 1 trimmed leek, cut into strips, and stir-fry for a further 2 minutes, then add 350 g (11½ oz) udon noodles and the reserved marinade, cover and cook for 2 minutes until the noodles are softened. Add the reserved chicken to the wok, toss together well and heat through.

30 Roast Pork Loin with Creamy Cabbage and Leeks

Serves 4

1 teaspoon ground cumin

1 teaspoon ground coriander

500 g (1 lb) pork loin, trimmed of fat

3 tablespoons olive oil

300 g (10 oz) sweet potatoes, peeled and chopped

250 g (8 oz) savoy cabbage, shredded

3 leeks, trimmed and sliced

3 tablespoons soured cream

2 teaspoons wholegrain mustard

• Mix together the spices in a bowl, then rub over the pork. Heat 1 tablespoon of the oil in an ovenproof frying pan, add the pork and cook until browned on all sides. Transfer to a preheated oven, 180°C (350°F), Gas Mark 4, and cook for 20–25 minutes or until cooked through. Leave to rest for 2 minutes.

• Meanwhile, cook the sweet potatoes in a saucepan of boiling water for 12–15 minutes until tender, adding the cabbage and leeks 3–4 minutes before the end of the cooking time. Drain well.

• Heat the remaining oil in a frying pan, add the vegetables and fry for 7–8 minutes until starting to turn golden. Stir in the cream and mustard.

• Slice the pork and serve on top of the vegetables.

---

1 **Grilled Pork Chops with Cabbage and Leek Mash** Cook 4 pork chops, about 150 g (5 oz) each, under a preheated hot grill for 5 minutes on each side or until cooked through. Meanwhile, cook 500 g (1 lb) peeled and finely diced potatoes, ½ finely shredded savoy cabbage and 2 trimmed and finely sliced leeks in a saucepan of boiling water for 8 minutes until tender. Drain, then mash in the pan with 2 tablespoons natural yogurt and salt and pepper. Serve with the pork.

2 **Pork Steaks with Cabbage and Leek Potato Cakes** Cook 500 g (1 lb) peeled and diced potatoes in a saucepan of boiling water for 8–10 minutes until tender. Meanwhile, heat 1 tablespoon olive oil in a frying pan, add ½ finely shredded cabbage and 1 trimmed and diced leek and cook for 3–4 minutes until soft. Drain the potatoes, return to the pan and mash. Stir in the cabbage and leeks and transfer to a bowl to cool slightly. Shape into 8 rounds, then dredge with a little flour. Melt 50 g (2 oz) butter with the juice of ½ lemon and 1 crushed garlic clove in a frying pan. Brush 4 pork steaks, about 150 g (5 oz) each, with the butter, then cook under a preheated hot grill for 3–4 minutes on each side or until cooked through. Meanwhile, heat 2 tablespoons olive oil in a separate pan, add the potato cakes and cook for 2–3 minutes on each side. Serve with the pork.

30 Nectarine-Glazed Chicken Kebabs

Serves 4

2 nectarines, halved, stoned and roughly chopped

4-cm (1½-inch) piece of fresh root ginger, peeled and roughly chopped

2 garlic cloves, chopped

1 teaspoon soy sauce

1 teaspoon Worcestershire sauce

2 teaspoons olive oil

600 g (1¼ lb) chicken breast fillets, cut into bite-sized pieces

1 red pepper, cored, deseeded and cut into bite-sized pieces

1 yellow pepper, cored, deseeded and cut into bite-sized pieces

crisp green salad, to serve

- Place the nectarines, ginger, garlic, soy sauce, Worcestershire sauce and oil in a small food processor or blender and blitz until completely smooth.

- Place the chicken and peppers in a non-metallic bowl and pour over the marinade. Cover and leave to marinate in the refrigerator for 5 minutes.

- Thread the pieces of chicken and pepper on to metal skewers and cook under a preheated medium grill or on the barbecue for 12–15 minutes, turning frequently, or until the chicken is cooked through.

- Serve with a crisp green salad.

---

1 Chicken and Nectarine Salad

Whisk together 1 tablespoon white wine vinegar, 3 tablespoons olive oil, 1 tablespoon chopped mint, 1 teaspoon honey and ½ teaspoon Dijon mustard in a bowl. Toss together 3 halved, stoned and sliced nectarines, 400 g (13 oz) shop-bought ready-cooked chicken breast, cubed, 1 chopped cucumber, ½ sliced red onion and 50 g (2 oz) rocket leaves in a serving bowl. Toss with the dressing and serve with crusty bread.

2 Chicken Satay with Nectarine Salad

Soak 16 wooden skewers in water for 10 minutes. Meanwhile, cut 500 g (1 lb) chicken breast fillets into strips, then lay on a board, cover with clingfilm and bash with a meat mallet or rolling pin to flatten slightly. Mix together 3 tablespoons soy sauce, 1 tablespoon vegetable oil, 1 tablespoon lime juice, 1 teaspoon each of ground cumin and ground coriander and 2 crushed garlic cloves in a non-metallic bowl. Add the chicken and mix to coat well, then cover and leave to marinate in the refrigerator for 5 minutes. Mix together 1 tablespoon oyster sauce, 1 tablespoon crunchy peanut butter, 3 tablespoons sweet chilli sauce and the juice of ½ lime in a small bowl. Using a vegetable peeler, slice 1 cucumber into long, thin strips and place on a serving plate with 2 halved, stoned and thinly sliced nectarines. Thread the chicken strips on to the skewers, then cook under a preheated hot grill or on a barbecue for 2 minutes on each side or until cooked through. Serve with the cucumber salad and the peanut sauce for dipping.

20 Calves' Liver with Caramelized Onions

Serves 4

3 tablespoons olive oil
1 large onion, finely sliced
4 teaspoons balsamic vinegar
1 teaspoon caster sugar
650 g (1 lb 7 oz) potatoes, peeled
  and chopped
500 g (1 lb) sweet potatoes,
  peeled and chopped
2 tablespoons plain flour
½ tablespoon freshly ground
  black pepper
500 g (1 lb) calves' liver, cut into
  strips
20 g (¾ oz) butter
20 g (¾ oz) rocket leaves
salt and pepper

- Heat 1 tablespoon of the oil in a frying pan, add the onion and sauté over a medium heat for about 5 minutes. Add the vinegar and sugar and cook for a further 15 minutes, stirring occasionally, until caramelized.

- Meanwhile, cook the potatoes and sweet potatoes in a saucepan of boiling water for 12–15 minutes until tender.

- Mix together the flour and pepper on a plate. Toss the liver in the flour to coat. Heat the remaining oil in a separate frying pan, add the liver and cook over a high heat for 2–3 minutes on each side until golden, taking care not to overcook it.

- Drain the potatoes, then return to the pan and mash with the butter and salt and pepper. Stir in the rocket, then serve with the liver and onions.

---

10 **Calves' Liver Pâté with Caramelized Onion** Heat 175 g (6 oz) butter in a frying pan, add 1 large chopped onion and 2 crushed garlic cloves and cook for 2–3 minutes. Add 375 g (12 oz) chopped calves' liver and 4 finely chopped streaky bacon rashers and cook over a medium heat for 4–5 minutes. Tip into a food processor with a dash of Worcestershire sauce, a pinch of nutmeg and 2 teaspoons thyme leaves and blitz until smooth. Serve on toasted slices of baguette with ready-made caramelized onion.

30 **Calves' Liver with Caramelized Shallot Sauce** Melt 25 g (1 oz) butter in a frying pan, add 2 finely chopped shallots and cook over a low heat for 10 minutes, then add 1 tablespoon capers, rinsed and drained, and 175 ml (6 fl oz) sherry and simmer until reduced by half. Stir in 2 teaspoons sherry vinegar, 150 ml (¼ pint) beef stock and 25 g (1 oz) butter and whisk until starting to thicken. Stir in 1 tablespoon chopped sage. Meanwhile, cook 625 g (1¼ lb) peeled and chopped potatoes in a saucepan of boiling water for 15–16 minutes until tender. Heat 1 tablespoon olive oil in a separate large frying pan, add 4 pieces of calves' liver, about 175 g (6 oz) each, and cook over a high heat for 2–3 minutes on each side. Drain the potatoes, then mash in the pan with 1 tablespoon natural yogurt and salt and pepper. Serve with the liver, with the sauce poured over.

1  Coronation Chicken with Avocado Salad

Serves 4

150 g (5 oz) mayonnaise
1½ teaspoons mild curry powder
1 teaspoon ground allspice
1 red chilli, deseeded and diced
juice of ½ lime
6 tablespoons mango chutney
6 tablespoons Greek yogurt
550 g (1 lb 2 oz) shop-bought
   ready-cooked chicken, shredded
½ iceburg lettuce, leaves torn
30 g (1 oz) watercress
2 avocados, peeled and sliced
2 large beef tomatoes, sliced
2 tablespoons toasted flaked
   almonds

- Mix together the mayonnaise, curry powder, allspice, chilli, lime juice, chutney and yogurt in a large bowl, then stir in the chicken.

- Place the lettuce on a serving plate, then top with the watercress, avocados and tomatoes.

- Spoon over the chicken and serve sprinkled with the almonds.

2 Chicken Kebabs with Avocado Dip

Grind 2 garlic cloves, 1 tablespoon grated ginger and 3 chopped spring onions to a paste. Stir in the juice of ½ lime, 1 tablespoon soy sauce and 1 tablespoon oil. Place 625 g (1¼ lb) cubed chicken breast and 20 button mushrooms in bowl, pour over the marinade and toss. Thread the chicken, mushrooms and 20 cherry tomatoes on to 16 metal skewers. Cook in a preheated hot griddle pan for 7–8 minutes on each side until cooked through. Meanwhile, mix together 2 peeled and mashed avocados, the juice of ½ lemon, 2 chopped tomatoes and a pinch of chilli flakes. Serve with the kebabs.

3 Coconut Chicken with Avocado

Salsa Mix together 2 peeled, stoned and diced avocados, 2 diced tomatoes, ½ diced red onion, 1 tablespoon chopped coriander and the juice of ½ lime in a bowl, then leave to stand. Meanwhile, place 3 shallots, 3 garlic cloves, 1–2 halved and deseeded red chillies, 1 lemon grass stalk and 1 teaspoon each of turmeric and peeled and grated fresh root ginger in a food processor and whizz to a paste. Heat 2 tablespoons peanut oil in a wok or large frying pan and cook the paste for 4–5 minutes. Pour in a 400 ml (14 fl oz) can coconut milk and bring to a simmer. Add 4 boneless, skinless chicken breasts, about 150 g (5 oz) each, and simmer for 10–12 minutes. Remove the chicken from the broth with a slotted spoon and cook on a barbecue or under a preheated hot grill for 6–8 minutes, turning once, until cooked through. Serve with the broth, cooked rice and the avocado salsa.

Stir-Fried Beef and Leeks

Serves 4

2 tablespoons sunflower oil
400 g (13 oz) sirloin steak, cut
    into strips
2 garlic cloves, crushed
1 teaspoon dried chilli flakes
4 leeks, trimmed and thinly sliced
juice of 1 lemon
2 tablespoons crème fraîche
salt and pepper
steamed broccoli, to serve

· Heat the oil in a wok or large frying pan until hot, add the beef and stir-fry for 2 minutes. Remove from the pan with a slotted spoon.

· Add the garlic, chilli flakes and leeks to the pan and stir-fry for 3–4 minutes.

· Return the beef to the pan, stir in the lemon juice and crème fraiche and cook for 2 minutes until heated through.

· Season to taste and serve with steamed broccoli.

Beef Steak and Caramelized Leek

Sandwiches Heat 25 g (1 oz) butter and 1 tablespoon olive oil in a frying pan, add 2 trimmed and sliced leeks and cook over a low heat for 10 minutes, stirring occasionally. Add 1 tablespoon brown sugar and 1 tablespoon white wine and cook for a further 5 minutes. Meanwhile, heat a griddle pan until hot, add 4 sirloin steaks, about 150 g (5 oz) each, and cook for 3–4 minutes on each side, or until cooked to your liking. Leave to rest. Toast 4 halved ciabatta rolls, then spread the bases with 1 teaspoon horseradish mixed with 1 tablespoon mayonnaise. Top each with a steak and the caramelized leeks, then add the lids and serve.

Beef and Leek Filo Pie

Heat 1 tablespoon olive oil in a frying pan, add 400 g (13 oz) chopped steak and cook for 8 minutes. Stir in 3 trimmed and sliced leeks and cook for a further 4 minutes. Sprinkle over 1 tablespoon plain flour and cook for 1 minute, then pour in 125 ml (4 fl oz) white wine. Simmer for 4 minutes, then stir in 100 g (3½ oz) cream cheese and 2 tablespoons chopped parsley. Spoon into an ovenproof dish. Brush the edges of the dish with olive oil, then lay 1 sheet of filo pastry over the top. Brush with olive oil, then lay another sheet on top. Scrunch up the over-hanging pastry on to the top of the pie and drizzle with a little more olive oil. Bake for 12 minutes in a preheated oven, 190°C (375°F), Gas Mark 5, until golden. Serve with steamed vegetables.

10 Chicken Liver Salad with Mustard Dressing

Serves 4

200 g (7 oz) streaky bacon
  rashers
5 tablespoons olive oil
200 g (7 oz) crusty bread,
  cut into small cubes
400 g (13 oz) chicken livers,
  halved and trimmed
25 g (1 oz) watercress
50 g (2 oz) lamb's lettuce
3 small ready-cooked fresh
  beetroot, cut into wedges
1 red onion, sliced
1 tablespoon raspberry vinegar
1 tablespoon Dijon mustard
1 teaspoon honey

- Cook the bacon under a preheated hot grill for 6–8 minutes until crisp.

- Meanwhile, heat 1 tablespoon of the oil in a frying pan, add the bread and cook for 3–4 minutes, turning frequently, until golden. Remove from the pan with a slotted spoon and drain on kitchen paper.

- Heat another tablespoon of the oil in the pan and cook the chicken livers for 2–3 minutes on each side, until golden brown but still slightly pink in the middle. Leave to cool slightly, then cut into bite-sized pieces.

- Toss together the watercress, lamb's lettuce, beetroot and onion in a serving bowl, then add the chicken livers and croûtons. Top with the bacon.

- Whisk together the remaining oil, vinegar, mustard and honey in a small bowl and drizzle over the salad to serve.

20 Chicken Liver and Mustard Pâté

Heat 100 g (3½ oz) butter over a medium heat, add 1 diced onion and cook for 3–4 minutes. Add 1 crushed garlic clove and 450 g (14½ oz) trimmed and halved chicken livers and fry for 6–8 minutes until cooked through. Stir in 1 tablespoon brandy and 1 teaspoon mustard powder and season well. Tip into a food processor with 65 g (2½ oz) melted butter and blitz until smooth. Pour into 4 small ramekins and leave to cool before serving.

30 Chicken Livers with Mustard Mash

Heat 1 tablespoon olive oil in a frying pan, add 3 thinly sliced onions and cook over a low heat for 20 minutes, stirring occasionally. Pour in 2 tablespoons Madeira wine and 2 teaspoons sugar and cook for a further 5–6 minutes until caramelized. Meanwhile, cook 750 g (1½ lb) peeled and chopped potatoes in a saucepan of boiling water for 12–15 minutes until tender. Heat 1 tablespoon olive oil in a separate frying pan and cook 450 g (14½ oz) trimmed and halved chicken livers for 2–3 minutes on each side until just cooked through. Drain the potatoes and mash in the pan with 2 tablespoons wholegrain mustard, 25 g (1 oz) butter, 1 tablespoon soured cream and salt and pepper. Serve the mash topped with the chicken livers and caramelized onions.

QuickCook
Fish and Seafood

Recipes listed by cooking time

30

2

20 Moules Marinières

Serves 4

40 g (1¾ oz) butter
3 shallots, chopped
2 garlic cloves, crushed
50 ml (2 fl oz) white wine
2 kg (4 lb) mussels, scrubbed
  and debearded
100 ml (3½ fl oz) single cream
2–3 tablespoons chopped parsley
crusty bread, to serve

· Melt the butter in a large saucepan, add the shallots and garlic and cook for 3–4 minutes until softened. Pour in the wine and bring to the boil.

· Add the mussels (first discarding any that don't shut when tapped against a work surface), cover the pan and cook for 3–4 minutes, shaking the pan once or twice, until all the shells are open. Discard any mussels that remain shut.

· Stir in the cream and parsley and heat through.

· Serve in deep bowls with crusty bread to mop up the juices.

10 Smoked Mussel Bruschetta

Cut 1 baguette into 8 thick slices. Drizzle with olive oil, then toast under a preheated hot grill for 2–3 minutes on each side until golden. Meanwhile, toss together 2 diced tomatoes, a small handful of chopped watercress, 4 sliced spring onions and 125 g (4 oz) smoked mussels in a bowl. Rub one side of each slice of toast with a garlic clove, then top with the mussels. Serve sprinkled with grated Pecorino cheese.

30 Mussel and Watercress

Linguine Place 100 ml (3½ fl oz) white wine and 1.5 kg (3 lb) scrubbed and debearded mussels (first discarding any that don't shut when tapped against a work surface) in a large saucepan, cover and cook for 3–4 minutes until all the shells are open. Discard any mussels that remain shut. Drain, then remove the mussels from the shells. Heat 3 tablespoons olive oil in a frying pan, add 2 diced shallots and 2 crushed garlic cloves and cook for 2–3 minutes. Stir in 2 tablespoons ready-made pesto. Cook 400 g (13 oz) linguine in a saucepan of boiling water for 8–9 minutes, or according to the pack instructions, until 'al dente'. Add the mussels to the pesto mixture with 80 g (3 oz) roughly chopped watercress. Drain the pasta, then toss in the sauce. Serve sprinkled with Parmesan cheese shavings.

30 Oysters Rockefeller

Serves 4

3 tablespoons olive oil

1 shallot, diced

1 garlic clove, crushed

175 g (6 oz) baby spinach leaves

dash of Pernod (optional)

24 oysters, opened and in the half-shells

100 g (3½ oz) fresh wholemeal breadcrumbs

100 g (3½ oz) Parmesan cheese, grated

rock salt

- Heat 2 tablespoons of the oil in a frying pan, add the shallot and garlic and cook for 2–3 minutes. Add the spinach and stir until wilted. Add the Pernod, if using, and cook until the liquid has been absorbed.

- Cover the base of a roasting tin with rock salt, then arrange the oysters on top. Spoon the spinach mixture on to the oysters. Mix together the breadcrumbs and cheese, then sprinkle over the spinach.

- Drizzle with the remaining oil and bake in a preheated oven, 200°C (400°F), Gas Mark 6, for 10–15 minutes until lightly golden.

1 Oysters with Shallot Vinaigrette

Mix together 2 finely diced shallots, 4 tablespoons sherry vinegar, 4 tablespoons olive oil, the juice of 1 lemon and 2 tablespoons chopped parsley in a bowl. Spoon over 24 shucked oysters and serve.

2 Oysters Kilpatrick

Heat ½ tablespoon olive oil in a frying pan, add 100 g (3½ oz) bacon lardons and cook for 3–4 minutes until crisp. Remove from the pan with a slotted spoon and drain on kitchen paper. Melt 20 g (¾ oz) butter in the frying pan, add 2 diced shallots and fry for 2 minutes, then remove the pan from the heat and add 2 tablespoons Worcestershire sauce, 2 tablespoons tomato ketchup and a few drops of Tabasco. Shuck 24 oysters, return to the half-shells and place on a baking sheet. Spoon over the sauce and scatter over the bacon. Cook under a preheated hot grill for 1–2 minutes until just cooked through and sizzling. Serve with lemon wedges.

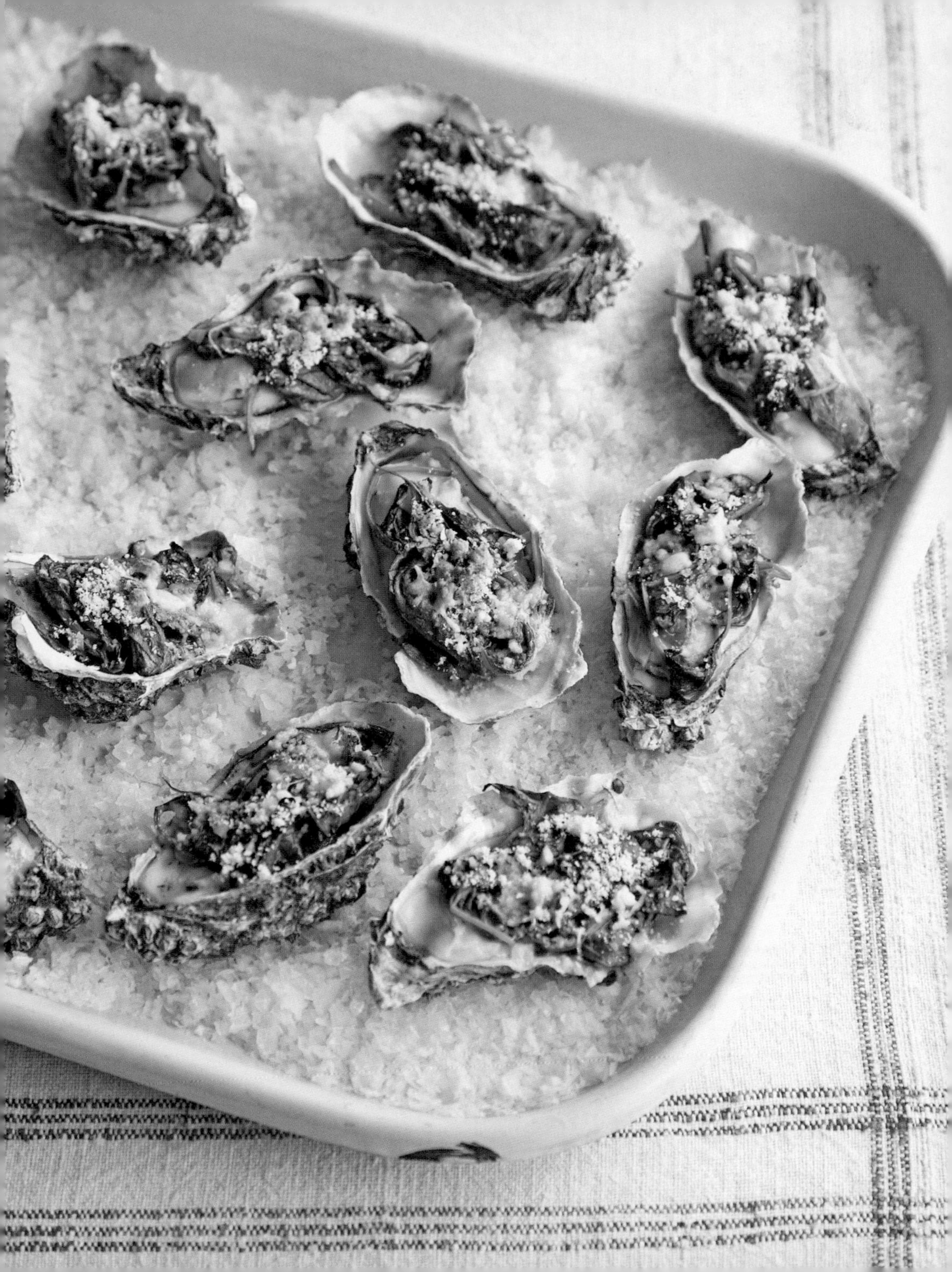

10 Salmon and Rice Bhajis

Serves 4

2 x 170 g (6 oz) cans salmon, drained and flaked
1 small onion, sliced
½ teaspoon ground cumin
¼ teaspoon dried chilli flakes
2 tablespoons chopped coriander
75 g (3 oz) ready-cooked white rice
1 egg, beaten
1–2 tablespoons plain flour
2 tablespoons rapeseed oil
150 g (5 oz) natural yogurt
½ cucumber, grated
1 tablespoon chopped mint
salt and pepper

- Place the salmon, onion, spices, coriander and rice in a large bowl and mix well. Stir in the egg and season well. Mix in enough of the flour to form a stiff mixture. Using wet hands, shape into 20 small balls.

- Heat the oil in a large frying pan, add the bhajis and fry for 3–4 minutes, turning once, until golden.

- Meanwhile, mix together the yogurt, cucumber and mint in a bowl. Serve with the bhajis.

2 Salmon and Rice Salad

Place 4 skinless 150 g (5 oz) salmon fillets in a shallow non-metallic dish. Pour over 5 tablespoons sweet chilli sauce and the juice of 1 lime, cover and marinate for 10 minutes. Meanwhile, cook 200 g (7 oz) basmati rice in boiling water for 10–12 minutes, or according to the pack instructions, until tender. Drain, then stir in 2 tablespoons white wine vinegar and 1 tablespoon sugar. Cook the salmon under a preheated hot grill for 4–5 minutes on each side. Flake into chunks in a serving bowl, then stir in the rice, 2 carrots, cut into matchsticks, 4 shredded spring onions and 1 deseeded and shredded red chilli. Serve with lime wedges.

3 Marinated Salmon with Ginger Rice

Mix together 2 tablespoons soy sauce, 1 tablespoon white wine vinegar, 1 tablespoon honey, ½ tablespoon mustard and 2 crushed garlic cloves in a non-metallic dish. Add 4 skinless salmon fillets, about 150 g (5 oz) each, cover and leave to marinate in the refrigerator for 20 minutes, turning the salmon after 10 minutes. Meanwhile, heat 1 tablespoon coconut oil in a frying pan, add 2 sliced onions and fry for 3–4 minutes until slightly browned. Stir in a 2.5-cm (1-inch) piece of fresh root ginger, peeled and chopped, and 1 thinly sliced garlic clove and cook for a further minute.

Stir in 200 g (7 oz) basmati rice, then pour over 600 ml (1 pint) boiling water. Cover and cook for 10–12 minutes until the rice is tender. Cook the salmon fillets under a preheated hot grill for 4–5 minutes on each side or until just cooked through, basting with the marinade. Serve with the rice, sprinkled with a small handful of torn coriander leaves.

Smoked Mackerel and New Potato Salad

Serves 4

750 g (1½ lb) new potatoes, halved if large
200 g (7 oz) crème fraîche
2 teaspoons creamed horseradish
juice of 1 lemon
2 tablespoons pumpkin seeds
4 smoked mackerel fillets, about 100 g (3½ oz) each, skinned and flaked
175 g (6 oz) watercress
salt and pepper

- Cook the potatoes in a saucepan of boiling water for 15–16 minutes until tender.

- Meanwhile, mix together the crème fraîche, horseradish and lemon juice in a large serving bowl and season to taste.

- Heat a nonstick frying pan over a medium-low heat and dry-fry the pumpkin seeds for 2–3 minutes, stirring frequently, until golden brown and toasted. Set aside.

- Drain the potatoes, then refresh under cold running water and drain again. Mix with the crème fraîche mixture. Gently toss in the mackerel and watercress.

- Serve sprinkled with the toasted pumpkin seeds.

Smoked Mackerel Dip

Skin and flake 500 g (1 lb) smoked mackerel fillets into a bowl. Mix in 6–7 chopped spring onions, 275 g (9 oz) crème fraîche, the juice of ½ lemon and 2–3 teaspoons creamed horseradish. Season to taste with salt and pepper and serve with vegetable crudités and toasted pitta breads.

Pan-Fried Mackerel with Crushed Potatoes

Cook 1 kg (2 lb) peeled and chopped potatoes in a saucepan of boiling water for 12–15 minutes until tender. Drain the potatoes, then return to the pan and stir in a small handful of chopped parsley, 2 teaspoons creamed horseradish, 2 teaspoons wholegrain mustard and 2 tablespoons chopped chives. Crush the potatoes lightly with a masher or the back of a fork. Cover and keep warm. Heat 1 tablespoon olive oil in a frying pan, add 4 fresh mackerel fillets and cook for 3–4 minutes on each side or until cooked through. Spoon the crushed potatoes on to 4 plates, top with the mackerel and drizzle with 2 tablespoons olive oil.

3 0 Salmon Ceviche

Serves 4

450 g (14½ oz) very fresh salmon
  fillet, skinned and thinly sliced
juice of 6–8 limes
4 spring onions, finely chopped
2 celery sticks, finely sliced
1 tablespoon finely chopped
  coriander
lime wedges, to serve

- Place the salmon in a non-metallic bowl and cover with the lime juice. Cover and leave to marinate in the refrigerator for 20 minutes.

- Drain the lime juice from the salmon, then add the spring onions, celery and coriander and mix well.

- Serve with lime wedges.

---

1 0 Smoked Salmon Blinis

Heat through 16 ready-made blinis according to the pack instructions. Meanwhile, mix together 5 tablespoons crème fraîche and 1 tablespoon creamed horseradish in a bowl. Spoon a little of the horseradish cream on to each blini and top with 10 g (⅓oz) smoked salmon and a dill sprig. Season with pepper and serve.

2 0 Hot-Smoked Salmon and Potato Salad

Cook 250 g (8 oz) halved new potatoes in a saucepan of boiling water for 12 minutes until tender, adding 100 g (3½ oz) asparagus tips 2 minutes before the end of the cooking time. Drain, refresh under cold running water and drain again, then place in a large bowl. Whisk together the juice of 1 lemon, 3 tablespoons olive oil, 1 teaspoon each of wholegrain mustard and honey and 1 deseeded and diced red chilli in a small bowl. Add 125 g (4 oz) salad leaves, 4 sliced spring onions, 2 tablespoons chopped parsley and 375 g (12 oz) flaked hot-smoked salmon fillets to the potatoes. Add the dressing and lightly toss together before serving.

Baked Plaice with Mushrooms and Hazelnuts

Serves 4

2 tablespoons rapeseed oil
75 g (3 oz) chestnut mushrooms, chopped
75 g (3 oz) roasted chopped hazelnuts
½ tablespoon chopped parsley
4 plaice fillets, skinned
4 tablespoons white wine
25 g (1 oz) butter
400 g (13 oz) new potatoes, halved
1 tablespoon chopped mint
4 Little Gem lettuces, quartered
pepper

- Heat 1 tablespoon of the oil in a frying pan, add the mushrooms and cook for 5 minutes until softened. Stir in the hazelnuts, then remove from the heat and stir in the parsley.

- Lay the plaice fillets on a clean surface and divide the mushroom mixture between them, then roll up to enclose the stuffing. Place each fillet on a piece of foil large enough to enclose it, sprinkle with the white wine, season with pepper, add a knob of butter and wrap well. Bake in a preheated oven, 200°C (400°F), Gas Mark 6, for 15 minutes or until cooked through.

- Heat the remaining oil in a frying pan, add the lettuce and fry for 2–3 minutes on each side.

- Meanwhile, cook the potatoes in a saucepan of boiling water for 12–15 minutes until tender. Drain and season, then add the mint and lightly crush with a fork. Serve the potatoes topped with the lettuce and plaice parcels.

---

1 Plaice with Caper Butter, Mushrooms and Hazelnut Green Salad Heat 2 tablespoons olive oil in a frying pan and sauté 100 g thinly sliced mushrooms for 1-2 minutes. Remove from the pan with a slotted spoon. Meanwhile, season 4 plaice fillets with salt and pepper, then dust each with 1 tablespoon flour. Heat 1 tablespoon olive oil in a frying pan, add the plaice fillets, skin side down, and fry for 3–4 minutes. Turn the fish over and cook for a further 1–2 minutes until cooked through. Remove from the pan and keep warm. Heat 100 g (3½ oz) butter and the grated rind of 1 lemon in the pan, stirring until the butter melts and becomes nutty brown. Remove from the heat and stir in the juice of 1 lemon, 4 tablespoons capers, rinsed and drained, and 3 tablespoons chopped parsley. Spoon the caper butter over the plaice fillets and serve with a crisp green salad tossed with the sautéed mushrooms and 20 g (¾ oz) roasted chopped hazelnuts.

2 Plaice with Mushroom Cream and Hazelnut Broccoli Put 4 plaice fillets in an ovenproof dish and cover with 225 g (7½ oz) sliced mushrooms. Sprinkle with the juice of 1 lemon and season. Dot with 25 g (1 oz) butter and bake in a preheated oven, 180°C (350°F), Gas Mark 4, for 16–17 minutes, basting frequently. Pour over 150 ml (¼ pint) single cream and brown under a preheated hot grill. Meanwhile, steam 350 g (11½ oz) Tenderstem broccoli for 3–4 minutes until tender. Toss together with 2 tablespoons olive oil and 3 tablespoons chopped hazelnuts. Serve with the plaice.

30 Cod Loin with Roasted Tomato Ratatouille

Serves 4

400 g (13 oz) courgettes, sliced
2 red peppers, cored, deseeded
 and chopped
2 red onions, cut into wedges
1 aubergine, chopped
4 garlic cloves, sliced
2 tablespoons olive oil
300 g (10 oz) cherry tomatoes
small handful of basil leaves, torn
4 cod loins, about 150 g (5 oz)
 each
salt and pepper

· Place the courgettes, red peppers, onions and aubergine in a roasting tin and toss together with the garlic, oil and salt and pepper. Place in a preheated oven, 220°C (425°F), Gas Mark 7, for 16 minutes.

· Add the tomatoes and basil to the vegetables and toss together. Nestle the cod loins among the vegetables, then return to the oven for a further 10–12 minutes or until the fish is cooked through.

---

1 Pan-Fried Cod Loin with Griddled Tomatoes and Veg Using a vegetable peeler, slice 3 courgettes into long, thin strips, then toss together with 1 tablespoon olive oil, 1 tablespoon chopped basil, 125 g (4 oz) asparagus tips and 150 g (5 oz) halved cherry tomatoes in a bowl. Cook the vegetables in a preheated hot griddle pan or on a barbecue until slightly charred. Meanwhile, heat 1 tablespoon olive oil in a frying pan, add 4 cod loins, about 150 g (5 oz) each, and cook for 3–4 minutes on each side or until cooked through. Serve with the chargrilled vegetables.

2 Baked Cod Loin, Tomatoes and Leeks Place 4 cod loins, about 150 g (5 oz) each, in a foil-lined ovenproof dish. Drizzle over 2 tablespoons olive oil and the juice of 1 lemon, then add 2 trimmed and sliced leeks and 100 g (3½ oz) halved cherry tomatoes and season with salt and pepper. Toss together gently, then seal the foil into a parcel. Place in a preheated oven, 200°C (400°F), Gas Mark 6, for 18–19 minutes or until the fish is cooked through. Meanwhile, cook 475 g (15 oz) peeled and chopped potatoes in a saucepan of boiling water for 12–15 minutes until tender. Drain, then mash in the pan with 1 tablespoon natural yogurt, ½ tablespoon olive oil and 4 sliced spring onions. Serve the cod with the mashed potatoes.

 Baked Sole with Fennel Pesto

Serves 4

1 fennel bulb, roughly chopped
2 tablespoons chopped dill
50 g (2 oz) toasted pine nuts
2 tablespoons ground almonds
50 g (2 oz) Parmesan cheese,
   grated
juice of ½ lemon
100 ml (3½ fl oz) olive oil, plus
   1 tablespoon for drizzling
4 lemon sole fillets, about 175 g
   (6 oz) each, skinned
2 courgettes
1 tablespoon olive oil
200 g (7 oz) green beans
2 tomatoes, chopped

- Place the fennel in a food processor and blend to a purée. Add the dill, pine nuts, ground almonds, cheese and lemon juice and blitz to combine. With the motor still running, slowly pour in the 100 ml (3½ fl oz) olive oil through the feed tube until combined.

- Place the sole fillets on a board, skinned side up, and spread with the fennel pesto. Using a vegetable peeler, slice the courgettes into long, thin strips, then place 2–3 slices on each sole fillet. Roll up the fish and place in an ovenproof dish.

- Drizzle with the remaining oil, cover and bake in a preheated oven, 190°C (375°F), Gas Mark 5, for 15 minutes until cooked through.

- Meanwhile, steam the green beans, then toss with the tomatoes and divide between 4 plates. Top each with a sole fillet and serve.

---

1 **Grilled Sole with Fennel Coleslaw**

Cook 4 sole fillets under a preheated hot grill for about 2–3 minutes on each side or until cooked through. Meanwhile, finely slice ½ red cabbage, 2 fennel bulbs, 1 celery stick and 1 apple, then mix with the juice of 1 lemon in a large bowl. Dry-fry 2 tablespoons walnuts in a nonstick frying pan for 3–4 minutes, stirring frequently, then add to the coleslaw with 2 tablespoons sultanas, 2 tablespoons natural yogurt and a pinch of cayenne pepper. Serve with the fish.

2 **Sole and Fennel Soup**

Heat 1 tablespoon olive oil in a large saucepan, add 1 chopped onion and 2 sliced garlic cloves and cook for 2 minutes until starting to soften. Add 2 thinly sliced fennel bulbs and cook for a further 8 minutes. Stir in 100 ml (3½ fl oz) white wine and cook for 2 minutes, then add 500 ml (17 fl oz) hot fish stock, 2 x 400 g (13 oz) cans chopped tomatoes and salt and pepper. Bring to the boil, then reduce the heat and simmer for 5 minutes. Add 625 g (1¼ lb) chopped skinned sole fillets and cook for 3 minutes or until cooked through. Stir in 2 tablespoons chopped parsley and serve with crusty bread.

20 Prawn and Spinach Curry

Serves 4

4 tomatoes
2 tablespoons groundnut oil
2 red onions, chopped
2.5-cm (1-inch) piece of fresh
 root ginger, peeled and grated
4 garlic cloves, sliced
¼ teaspoon chilli powder
½ teaspoon turmeric
1 teaspoon ground coriander
400 ml (14 fl oz) can coconut
 milk
150 g (5 oz) spinach, chopped
425 g (14 oz) raw peeled king
 prawns
1 tablespoon toasted flaked
 almonds
cooked basmati rice, to serve

- Place the tomatoes in a heatproof bowl and pour over boiling water to cover. Leave for 1–2 minutes, then drain, cut a cross at the stem end of each tomato and peel off the skins and chop.

- Heat the oil in a wok or large frying pan, add the onions, ginger and garlic and stir-fry for 2–3 minutes. Add the spices and cook for a further 2–3 minutes, then add the tomatoes.

- Pour in the coconut milk and bring to a simmer. Gradually add the spinach, stirring until wilted. Cook for 4–5 minutes.

- Stir in the prawns and cook for a further 2 minutes or until the prawns turn pink.

- Sprinkle with the almonds and serve with cooked rice.

10 Prawn Skewers with Spinach Salad

Thread 24 cooked peeled king prawns on to 8 metal skewers. Mix together 4 tablespoons each of soy sauce and tomato ketchup with 2 crushed garlic cloves in a bowl, then brush over the prawns. Cook under a preheated hot grill for 2–3 minutes on each side. Meanwhile, whisk together 3 tablespoons olive oil, the juice of ½ lemon, ½ teaspoon French mustard and ½ teaspoon honey in a large bowl. Add 2 handfuls of spinach, ½ sliced red onion, 2 peeled and sliced avocados and toss well. Serve with the skewers.

30 Prawn and Spinach Soufflés

Heat 1 tablespoon olive oil in a pan, add 225 g (7½ oz) baby spinach leaves and cook for 2–3 minutes until wilted. Meanwhile, melt 45 g (1¾ oz) butter in a small saucepan, then stir in 45 g (1¾ oz) plain flour to make a roux. Gradually whisk in 350 ml (12 fl oz) milk and cook, stirring continuously, for 2–3 minutes until the sauce is thick and smooth. Stir in 50 g (2 oz) grated Parmesan cheese, season and pour into a large bowl. Stir in the spinach and leave to cool for 3–4 minutes. Put 3 cooked peeled king prawns in each of 4 greased ramekins, then place on a baking sheet. Whisk 4 egg yolks into the spinach sauce. Whisk 4 egg whites in a clean bowl until stiff, then gently fold into the spinach mixture. Spoon into the ramekins, running a finger around the rim to help even rising. Sprinkle over 2 tablespoons grated Parmesan and bake in a preheated oven, 200°C (400°F), Gas Mark 6, for 20 minutes until risen and golden.

Grilled Lemon and Mustard Sardines

Serves 4
small handful of parsley leaves, chopped
1 tablespoon wholegrain mustard
juice of 1 lemon
8 sardines, boned, cleaned and gutted
2 tablespoons olive oil
lemon halves, to serve

- Mix together the parsley, mustard and lemon juice in a bowl, then spoon into the sardine cavities. Brush the fish with the oil.

- Cook under a preheated hot grill for 4 minutes on each side or until cooked through. Serve with lemon halves.

2 Sardine and Lemon Spaghetti

Cook 350 g (11½ oz) spaghetti in a saucepan of boiling water for 8–9 minutes, or according to the pack instructions, until 'al dente'. Meanwhile, heat 1 tablespoon olive oil in a frying pan, add ½ teaspoon mustard seeds and 3 sliced garlic cloves and cook for 1 minute. Stir in a pinch of dried chilli flakes, the grated rind of 1 lemon, 200 g (7 oz) canned chopped tomatoes and 2 x 90 g (3¼ oz) cans sardines in tomato sauce. Break up the sardines, then stir in 75 g (3 oz) pitted black olives, 1 tablespoon capers, rinsed and drained, and 2 tablespoons chopped parsley and heat through. Drain the pasta, toss in the sardine sauce and serve.

3 Lemony Sardine Fishcakes

Cook 625 g (1¼ lb) peeled and chopped potatoes in a saucepan of boiling water for 12–15 minutes until tender. Place 200 g (7 oz) spinach leaves in a saucepan with a small amount of water, then cover and cook until wilted. Drain, squeeze dry and roughly chop. Drain the potatoes, return to the pan and mash until smooth. Place in a bowl with the spinach and 2 drained 120 g (4 oz) cans sardines and gently mix together. Stir in 1 tablespoon chopped parsley, ½ tablespoon plain flour, the juice of ½ lemon and the grated rind of 1 lemon. Using wet hands, shape into patties. Heat 2 tablespoons groundnut oil in a frying pan, add the fishcakes and fry for 4–5 minutes on each side until golden. Meanwhile, mix together 3 tablespoons Greek yogurt, the juice of ½ lemon, 1 tablespoon chopped parsley and 3 tablespoons mayonnaise in a bowl. Serve the fishcakes with the yogurt dressing.

Smoked Haddock Omelettes

Serves 4

150 g (5 oz) smoked haddock
125 ml (4 fl oz) milk
12 eggs
50 g (2 oz) butter
200 g (7 oz) spinach leaves
salt and pepper

- Place the haddock and milk in a saucepan and poach the fish for 3–4 minutes or until cooked. Remove with a slotted spoon, then remove the skin and any bones. Flake the fish into a bowl.

- Beat the eggs in a separate large bowl and season.

- Heat a quarter of the butter in a frying pan until foaming, then pour in a quarter of the beaten egg. Stir a little with a fork, tipping the pan so the egg covers the base, then cook for 3–4 minutes until set.

- Place a quarter of the spinach on the omelette, then top with a quarter of the fish. Fold the omelette over and cook for a further minute. Serve on a warm plate.

- Repeat with the remaining ingredients.

---

1 Smoked Haddock with Poached Eggs

Place 4 smoked haddock fillets, about 150 g (5 oz) each, 1 bay leaf and 400 ml (14 fl oz) milk in a large frying pan and gently poach for 8–10 minutes or until cooked. Meanwhile, bring a saucepan of water to a gentle simmer and stir with a large spoon to create a swirl. Break 2 eggs into the water and cook for 3 minutes. Remove with a slotted spoon and keep warm. Repeat with another 2 eggs. Serve the fish topped with a poached egg and 1 tablespoon warmed ready-made hollandaise or mustard sauce.

2 Smoked Haddock with Soft-Boiled Eggs

Cook 1 kg (2 lb) peeled and chopped potatoes in a saucepan of boiling water for 12–15 minutes or until tender. Meanwhile, poach 4 smoked haddock fillets and 8 sliced spring onions with 400 ml (14 fl oz) milk (see left). Cook 4 eggs in a saucepan of boiling water for 4–5 minutes until softly boiled, then drain and cool slightly. Drain the potatoes, then mash in the pan with 1 tablespoon creamed horseradish and 2 teaspoons wholegrain mustard. Peel and halve the eggs. Serve the fish on the mustard mash, topped with the eggs and sprinkled with 1 tablespoon chopped chives.

20 Red Mullet with Warm Potato and Watercress Salad

Serves 4

500 g (1 lb) new potatoes, halved
2 tablespoons mayonnaise
1 tablespoon natural yogurt
2–3 teaspoons creamed horseradish
1 tablespoon chopped parsley
2 tablespoons olive oil
4 red mullet fillets
25 g (1 oz) watercress
salt and pepper

- Cook the potatoes in a saucepan of boiling water for 12–15 minutes until just tender.

- Meanwhile, mix together the mayonnaise, yogurt, horseradish and parsley in a large bowl, then season well.

- Heat the oil in a frying pan, add the red mullet and cook for 2–3 minutes on each side or until cooked through.

- Drain the potatoes, add to the mayonnaise mixture and mix well. Stir in the watercress.

- Divide the potato salad between 4 plates, then top with the fish, pouring the oil from the pan around the plates.

---

10 Red Mullet with Mango Salsa and Watercress Mix together 1 peeled, stoned and diced mango, ½ diced red onion, 2 diced tomatoes, ½ deseeded and diced red chilli, 1 tablespoon olive oil, ½ tablespoon balsamic vinegar and 1 tablespoon chopped coriander in a bowl. Heat 1 tablespoon olive oil in a frying pan, add 4 red mullet fillets and cook for 2–3 minutes on each side or until cooked through. Serve with the salsa and watercress.

30 Spiced Red Mullet with Lentil and Watercress Salad Heat 2 tablespoons coconut oil in a frying pan, add 1 diced red onion and cook for 2–3 minutes. Add 1 deseeded and diced green chilli, 1 cored, deseeded and diced yellow pepper and 1 cored and diced apple and cook for a further 2–3 minutes. Stir in a rinsed and drained 400 g (13 oz) can lentils, 2 diced tomatoes, 1 tablespoon toasted pine nuts, the juice of ½ lime and 2 tablespoons mint leaves and cook gently for 3–4 minutes. Transfer to a bowl and keep warm. Mix together 2 tablespoons plain flour and 1 teaspoon curry powder in a bowl, then dust 4 red mullet fillets with the spiced flour. Heat 1 tablespoon coconut oil in a frying pan, add the fish and cook for 2–3 minutes on each side or until cooked through. Remove from the pan and keep warm. Add 1 tablespoon raisins and a pinch each of turmeric and ground cumin to the pan and cook for 1–2 minutes, then pour in 200 ml (7 fl oz) coconut milk. Bring to a simmer and cook for 3–4 minutes. Remove from the heat and stir in the grated rind of ½ lemon. Stir 25 g (1 oz) chopped watercress into the lentil salad, then serve with the fish and the sauce spooned over.

Salmon and Grapefruit Salad

Serves 4

2 tablespoons pumpkin seeds

4 grapefruits

1 red pepper, cored, deseeded and sliced

4 spring onions, sliced

400 g (13 oz) can flageolet beans, rinsed and drained

2 avocados, peeled and sliced

2 handfuls of baby spinach leaves

300 g (10 oz) smoked salmon fillets, broken into large flakes

2 tablespoons olive oil

1 teaspoon honey

½ teaspoon Dijon mustard

- Heat a nonstick frying pan over a medium-low heat and dry-fry the pumpkin seeds for 2–3 minutes, stirring frequently, until golden and toasted. Set aside.

- Segment the grapefruits over a bowl to catch the juice. Place the segments in a separate bowl and add the red pepper, spring onions, flageolet beans, avocados, spinach and salmon.

- Add the oil, honey and mustard to the grapefruit juice and whisk together. Pour over the salad ingredients and toss together gently.

- Serve sprinkled with the toasted pumpkin seeds.

---

2 Breaded Salmon with Grapefruit

Heat 1 tablespoon olive oil in a frying pan, add 4 skinless salmon fillets, about 150 g (5 oz) each, and cook for 30 seconds on each side. Transfer the fish to a baking sheet and place in a preheated oven, 220°C (425°F), Gas Mark 7, for 3–4 minutes. Meanwhile, heat 1 tablespoon olive oil and 25 g (1 oz) butter in a frying pan, add 125 g (4 oz) fresh wholemeal breadcrumbs, 25 g (1 oz) mustard powder and 25 g (1 oz) chopped hazelnuts and cook for 2–3 minutes. Remove the fish from the oven and sprinkle over the breadcrumb mixture, then cook under a preheated hot grill for 2–3 minutes until the crisp and cooked through. Heat a little olive oil in a pan, add 500 g (1 lb) spinach leaves and cook until wilted, then divide between 4 plates. Top with the fish and the segments of 1 pink grapefruit.

3 Salmon with Grapefruit Dressing and Roasted Veg

Core, deseed and quarter 1 yellow and 2 red peppers then place in a roasting tin with 1 sliced aubergine and 1 sliced courgette. Drizzle with olive oil and cook in a preheated oven, 200°C (400°F), Gas Mark 6, for 16–18 minutes. Meanwhile, heat 1 tablespoon oil in a pan, add 4 skinless 150 g (5 oz) salmon fillets, and cook for 4–5 minutes on each side. Segment 1 pink grapefruit over a bowl to catch the juice, then chop the segments and add to the bowl. Stir in 200 ml (7 fl oz) natural yogurt and 2 tablespoons chopped mint. Serve the veg topped with the fish, with the dressing.

2 Keralan Fish Curry

Serves 4

1 red chilli, deseeded and chopped
1 teaspoon rapeseed oil
1 teaspoon ground coriander
½ teaspoon ground cumin
½ teaspoon turmeric
4 garlic cloves
2.5-cm (1-inch) piece of fresh
    root ginger, peeled and
    chopped
1 tablespoon coconut oil
¼ teaspoon fenugreek seeds
2 onions, finely sliced
125 ml (4 fl oz) coconut milk
300 ml (½ pint) water
400 g (13 oz) fresh mackerel
    fillets, skinned and cut into
    5-cm (2-inch) pieces
salt and pepper

- Place the chilli, rapeseed oil, ground coriander, cumin, turmeric, garlic and ginger in a mini food processor or small blender and blend to form a paste.

- Heat the coconut oil in a wok or large pan, add the paste and fenugreek seeds and fry for 2–3 minutes. Add the onions, coconut milk and measurement water, season and bring to the boil, then cook for about 5 minutes until reduced.

- Add the mackerel and simmer gently for 5–8 minutes or until cooked through.

1 Curried Fish Kebabs

Mix together
3 tablespoons natural yogurt,
1 teaspoon each of chopped garlic and ginger purée, the juice of ½ lime, 2 tablespoons curry paste and ½ teaspoon honey in a non-metallic bowl. Toss in 400 g (13 oz) chopped skinless salmon fillet and leave to marinate for 2–3 minutes. Thread the fish on to metal skewers, then cook on a barbecue or under a preheated hot grill for 2–3 minutes on each side or until cooked through. Serve with a crisp green salad.

3 Indian-Spiced Fishcakes

Cook 1 kg (2 lb) peeled and chopped potatoes in a saucepan of boiling water for 15–17 minutes until tender. Meanwhile, dry-fry 1 teaspoon cumin seeds in a nonstick frying pan for 2–3 minutes, stirring frequently, until toasted. Drain the potatoes, then mash in the pan with the toasted cumin seeds, 2 finely chopped spring onions, 1 deseeded and diced red chilli, 3 tablespoons chopped coriander and salt and pepper. Beat in 1 beaten egg, then carefully stir in 200 g (7 oz) flaked hot-smoked salmon fillets. Using wet hands, shape into 8 fishcakes, then coat in 4 tablespoons plain flour. Heat 25 g (1 oz) butter and 1 tablespooon sunflower oil in a frying pan, add the fishcakes and fry for about 2 minutes on each side until golden. Serve with yogurt raita and a rocket salad.

Smoked Haddock Welsh Rarebit

Serves 4

250 ml (8 fl oz) cider
50 g (2 oz) butter
50 g (2 oz) plain flour
250 g (8 oz) mature Cheddar
  cheese, grated
1½ teaspoons English mustard
1 tablespoon Worcestershire
  sauce
4 skinless smoked haddock fillets,
  about 150 g (5 oz) each
salt and pepper

To serve

50 g (2 oz) watercress
4 tomatoes, sliced

- Heat the cider in a small saucepan until warm.

- Melt the butter in a separate small saucepan, then stir in the flour to make a roux. Cook for 1–2 minutes, then gradually whisk in the cider and cook, stirring continuously, until the sauce is thick and smooth. Add the cheese, mustard and Worcestershire sauce and stir until the cheese has melted. Season to taste.

- Cook the haddock under a preheated hot grill for 3 minutes on each side or until just cooked through.

- Spoon the rarebit mixture on to the fish and grill for a further 2–3 minutes until bubbling and golden. Serve on a bed of watercress and sliced tomato.

Smoked Haddock and Tangy Cheese on Toast

Place 200 g (7 oz) skinless smoked haddock and 300 ml (½ pint) milk in a frying pan and gently poach for 2–3 minutes or until just cooked through, then remove any bones and break into large flakes. Meanwhile, toast 4 slices of wholemeal bread under a preheated hot grill for 2–3 minutes on each side. Spread one side of each slice with ½ tablespoon mango chutney, then top with the flaked fish. Sprinkle with 4–5 tablespoons grated mature Cheddar cheese. Grill for 2–3 minutes until bubbling and golden.

Smoked Mackerel and Cheese Toasts

Place 4 sliced ripe tomatoes on a serving plate, then scatter over ½ thinly sliced red onion. Drizzle with 1 tablespoon vinaigrette and leave to stand. Skin and flake 2 smoked mackerel fillets into a bowl, then mix together with 4 tablespoons natural yogurt, 50 g (2 oz) grated Parmesan cheese, 1 teaspoon creamed horseradish and 1 tablespoon chopped chives. Bring a saucepan of water to a gentle simmer and stir with a large spoon to create a swirl. Break 2 eggs into the water and cook for 3 minutes. Remove with a slotted spoon and keep warm.

Repeat with another 2 eggs. Toast 4 thick slices of granary bread under a preheated hot grill for 2–3 minutes on each side. Spoon over the fish mixture and sprinkle with 50 g (2 oz) grated Parmesan. Grill for 3–4 minutes until bubbling, then top with the poached eggs and serve with the tomato salad.

King Prawn Caesar Salad

Serves 4

1 tablespoon olive oil
2 slices of white bread, crusts
removed, cut into small squares
2 garlic cloves
4 anchovy fillets in oil, drained
2 teaspoons lemon juice
1 teaspoon Dijon mustard
½ teaspoon Worcestershire sauce
200 ml (7 fl oz) natural yogurt
1 large romaine lettuce, torn
250 g (8 oz) cooked peeled
king prawns
15 g (½ oz) Parmesan cheese,
grated

- To make the croûtons, heat the oil in a frying pan until hot, then toss the bread in the pan for 3–4 minutes until golden. Remove with a slotted spoon and drain on kitchen paper.

- Place the garlic, anchovies, lemon juice, mustard, Worcestershire sauce and yogurt in a mini food processor or small blender and blend until smooth.

- Place the lettuce and prawns in a salad bowl with the croûtons, then add the yogurt mixture and cheese. Toss lightly to coat the salad with the dressing.

2 King Prawn Chilli Noodles

Heat 1 tablespoon coconut oil in a wok or frying pan, add 300 g (10 oz) raw peeled king prawns and stir-fry for 1–2 minutes or until they turn pink and are cooked through. Remove with a slotted spoon. Add 1 deseeded and chopped red chilli and 1 cored, deseeded and diced red pepper to the pan and stir-fry for 2 minutes, then add 150 g (5 oz) sugar snap peas and 4 sliced spring onions and stir-fry for a further 2 minutes. Stir in 2 tablespoons sweet chilli sauce, 1 tablespoon soy sauce and a pinch of sugar, then add 300 g (10 oz) straight-to-wok noodles and

100 ml (3½ fl oz) water and simmer for 2–3 minutes until the sauce is syrupy. Return the prawns to the pan and cook for 1 minute or until heated through. Serve sprinkled with 2 tablespoons chopped coriander.

3 King Prawn and Coconut Curry

Heat 1 tablespoon coconut oil in a wok or frying pan, add 2 grated onions and fry for 2–3 minutes, then add 1 teaspoon turmeric, 6 crushed cardamom pods, 1 teaspoon chilli powder, 3 crushed garlic cloves and 2 tablespoons peeled and grated root ginger and stir-fry for a further 1–2 minutes. Blend a small handful of coriander leaves and 300 ml (½ pint) coconut cream in a small blender, then stir into the onion mixture and bring to the boil. Reduce the heat and simmer for 15 minutes. Add 800 g (1¾ lb) raw peeled king prawns and cook for 3–4 minutes until they turn pink. Serve with cooked rice.

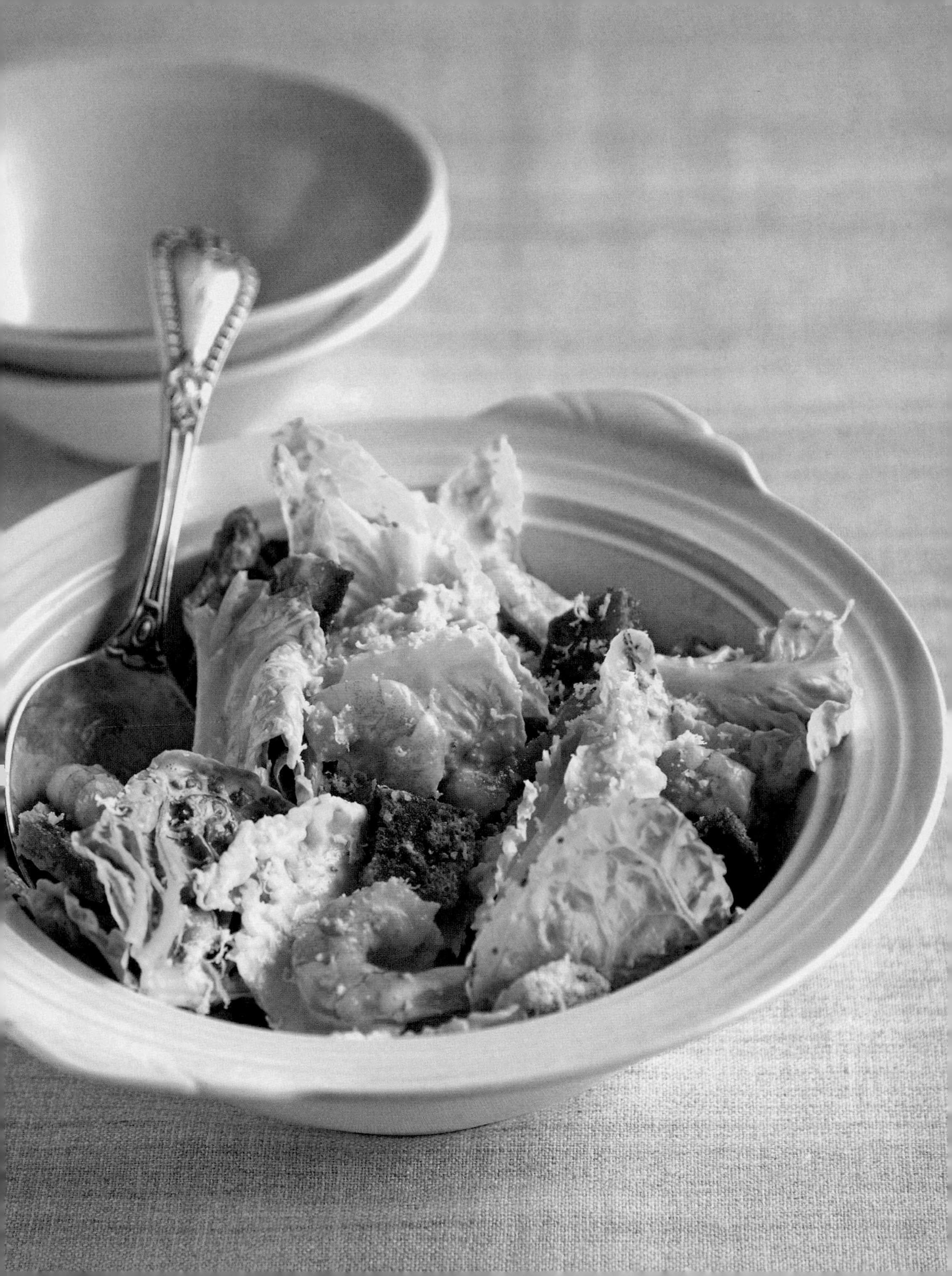

Smoked Mackerel and Spring Vegetable Tabbouleh

Serves 4

200 g (7 oz) couscous
150 g (5 oz) French beans, halved
100 g (3½ oz) fresh or frozen
  peas
150 g (5 oz) asparagus tips
4 spring onions, sliced
2 garlic cloves, finely diced
4 tablespoons chopped mint
4 tablespoons chopped parsley
3 peppered smoked mackerel
  fillets, skinned and flaked
3 tablespoons olive oil
juice of 1 lime
1 romaine lettuce, roughly torn
12 cherry tomatoes, halved
2 tablespoons toasted pine nuts
salt and pepper

- Place the couscous in a large heatproof bowl and just cover with boiling water. Leave to stand for 15 minutes.

- Meanwhile, steam or boil the French beans, peas and asparagus tips for 4–5 minutes until just tender. Refresh under cold running water and drain.

- Fluff up the couscous with a fork, then stir in the spring onions, garlic, herbs, mackerel, oil and lime juice. Season to taste.

- Arrange the lettuce and tomatoes on a serving plate, spoon over the couscous and sprinkle over the pine nuts.

Smoked Mackerel and Spring Vegetable Salad Lightly steam 150 g (5 oz) broccoli florets, 100 g (3½ oz) peas and 100 g (3½ oz) halved asparagus tips for 2–3 minutes, then refresh under cold running water and drain. Place in a large bowl with 2 chopped celery sticks, 4 sliced spring onions, 75 g (3 oz) halved green grapes, 3 skinned and flaked smoked mackerel fillets and 125 g (4 oz) cherry tomatoes. Toss with salad dressing and serve sprinkled with 2 tablespoons toasted flaked almonds.

Smoked Mackerel and Spring Vegetable Paella Heat 1 tablespoon olive oil in a large frying pan or paella pan, add 1 chopped onion and 2 crushed garlic cloves and cook for 1–2 minutes. Add 2 chopped courgettes and 2 peeled and diced carrots and cook for a further 1–2 minutes. Stir in 250 g (8 oz) paella rice and a 227 g (7½ oz) can chopped tomatoes. Stir in a pinch of paprika and a pinch of saffron threads, then pour in 900 ml (1½ pints) hot vegetable stock. Bring to the boil, then reduce the heat and simmer for 18–20 minutes until the rice is tender, adding 100 g (3½ oz) peas, 100 g (3½ oz) asparagus tips and 2 skinned and thinly sliced smoked mackerel fillets 2 minutes before the end of the cooking time. Stir in 2 tablespoons chopped parsley and season to taste.

Pan-Fried Sea Bass with Warm Leek and Lentil Salad

Serves 4

3 tablespoons olive oil
500 g (1 lb) leeks, trimmed and sliced
400 g (13 oz) can Puy lentils, rinsed and drained
3 teaspoons creamed horseradish
2 tablespoons crème fraîche
4 sea bass fillets
pepper

- Heat 1 tablespoon of the oil in a frying pan, add the leeks and season with pepper, then cook over a medium heat for 8–10 minutes until soft. Add the lentils and cook for a further 2–3 minutes. Stir in the horseradish and crème fraîche and continue to cook for 2–3 minutes.

- Meanwhile, heat 1 tablespoon of the oil in a frying pan, add the sea bass and cook for 3–4 minutes on each side or until cooked through.

- Serve the sea bass with the lentils, drizzled with the remaining oil.

Sea Bass, Leek and Lentil Soup

Heat 1 tablespoon coconut oil in a frying pan, add 1 chopped onion, 2 chopped garlic cloves and 3 trimmed and chopped leeks and cook for 3–4 minutes until softened. Stir in a rinsed and drained 400 g (13 oz) can green lentils and 1.2 litres (2 pints) hot vegetable stock and bring to the boil, then reduce the heat and simmer for 6 minutes, adding 250 g (8 oz) sea bass fillets, skinned and cut into bite-sized pieces, 2 minutes before the end of the cooking time. Season, stir in 2 tablespoons chopped parsley and serve.

Sea Bass with Spicy Leek and Lentil Bake

Heat 1 tablespoon olive oil in a frying pan, add 2 chopped onions and 1 crushed garlic clove and cook for 3–4 minutes until softened. Stir in 1 teaspoon peeled and grated fresh root ginger, 1 teaspoon garam masala and ½ teaspoon turmeric and cook for a further 1–2 minutes. Pour in 125 g (4 oz) rinsed and drained canned lentils and 375 ml (13 fl oz) hot vegetable stock and simmer for 2–3 minutes until all the liquid has been absorbed. Meanwhile, steam 4 trimmed leeks, cut into 2.5-cm (1-inch) lengths, for 4–5 minutes, then place in an ovenproof dish. Mash the lentils until smooth, then pour over the leeks and top with 2 tablespoons chopped walnuts. Bake in a preheated oven, 200°C (400°F), Gas Mark 6, for 18–20 minutes or until browned. Meanwhile, heat 1 tablespoon of olive oil in a frying pan, add 4 sea bass fillets, about 150 g (5 oz) each, and cook for 3–4 minutes on each side or until cooked through, then serve with the bake.

2 Grilled Salmon with Avocado Salsa

Serves 4

2 avocados, peeled, stoned
   and diced
juice of ½ lime
75 g (3 oz) baby plum tomatoes,
   diced
1 tablespoon chopped coriander
1 tablespoon olive oil
4 salmon fillets, about 150 g
   (5 oz) each

- Mix together the avocados and lime juice in a bowl to prevent discoloration. Add the tomatoes, coriander and oil and mix well. Leave to stand.

- Meanwhile, cook the salmon under a preheated medium grill, skin side up, for about 6–8 minutes until the skin starts to turn golden. Turn the fish over and cook for a further 4–5 minutes or until cooked through.

- Serve the salmon with a spoonful of salsa.

1 Salmon and Avocado Salad

Whisk together 3 tablespoons extra virgin olive oil, the grated rind and juice of 1 lemon, 1 teaspoon honey, ½ teaspoon Dijon mustard, 2 tablespoons shredded basil leaves and salt and pepper in a bowl. Using a vegetable peeler, slice 1 large courgette into long, thin strips and divide between 4 plates. Tear 500 g (1 lb) mozzarella cheese into chunks and divide between the plates, then top with 150 g (5 oz) smoked salmon, cut into strips, 75 g (3 oz) sun-dried tomatoes and 2 peeled, stoned and sliced avocados. Drizzle with the dressing and sprinkle with 2 tablespoons toasted pine nuts.

3 Salmon Parcels with Avocado

Sauce Place 2 avocados, 1 garlic clove, 1 teaspoon sherry vinegar and ½ teaspoon freshly ground black pepper in a food processor and blend until smooth. Place in a bowl and stir in 200 g (7 oz) crème fraîche. Cover and chill until required. Mix together 1 sliced red onion, 2 sliced garlic cloves, 2 chopped tomatoes, 1 teaspoon chopped dill and 100 ml (3½ fl oz) white wine. Place 4 skinless salmon fillets, about 150 g (5 oz) each, in a non-metallic bowl and pour over the marinade. Leave to stand for 5 minutes. Place the salmon and marinade in the centre of 4 large sheets of greaseproof paper, then fold up to make sealed packages. Place on a baking sheet and bake in a preheated oven, 200°C (400°F) Gas Mark 6, for 6–8 minutes or until cooked through. Serve with watercress and the avocado sauce.

30 Fish Pie

Serves 4

675 g (1 lb 9 oz) sweet potatoes,
  peeled and chopped
350 ml (12 fl oz) milk
125 g (4 oz) skinless salmon fillet,
  cut into bite-sized pieces
375 g (12 oz) cod loin or skinless
  cod fillet, cut into bite-size
  pieces
2 eggs
20 g (¾ oz) butter
1 tablespoon plain flour
½ teaspoon mustard
75 g (3 oz) baby spinach leaves
250 g (8 oz) cooked peeled king
  prawns
75 g (3 oz) Cheddar cheese,
  grated
pepper

- Cook the sweet potatoes in a saucepan of boiling water for 12 minutes or until tender.

- Meanwhile, pour the milk into a frying pan. Add the salmon and cod. Bring to a simmer and gently cook for 5–6 minutes or until the fish is just cooked through. Drain the fish, reserving the milk.

- Cook the eggs in a saucepan of boiling water for 4–5 minutes until softly boiled. Refresh under cold running water.

- Melt the butter in a small saucepan, then stir in the flour to make a roux. Cook for 1–2 minutes, then stir in the mustard. Gradually whisk in the reserved milk, and cook, stirring continuously, until the sauce is thick and smooth.

- Lay the spinach in an ovenproof dish and add the fish. Peel the eggs and cut into quarters, then place on the fish. Scatter in the prawns. Pour over the white sauce.

- Drain the sweet potatoes, then mash in the pan with plenty of pepper. Spoon over the fish and spread with a fork, then sprinkle with the cheese. Bake in a preheated oven, 200°C (400°F), Gas Mark 6, for 12–15 minutes until bubbling.

---

1 Fish Pâté

Chop 150 g (5 oz) smoked salmon into small pieces. Place 200 g (7 oz) cream cheese, 1 tablespoon natural yogurt, the juice of ½ lemon and salt and pepper in a food processor and blitz until smooth. Add the salmon and pulse to form a chunky pâté. Stir in a small bunch of chopped dill or chives. Serve with warm toast or breadsticks.

2 Fish Soup

Heat 2 tablespoons olive oil in a large saucepan, add 1 chopped onion, 1 chopped fennel bulb, 2 crushed garlic cloves and ½ teaspoon fennel seeds and cook for 2–3 minutes. Stir in a 400 g (13 oz) can chopped tomatoes and cook for a further 6–8 minutes. Pour in 2 litres (3½ pints) hot fish stock and a pinch of saffron threads and bring to the boil. Add 250 g (8 oz) cooked peeled prawns, 250 g (8 oz) live clams, cleaned, and 400 g (13 oz) skinless salmon fillet, cut into bite-sized pieces, and simmer for 5–6 minutes or until the fish is cooked through and the clams have opened. Discard any shells that remain shut. Add 2 tablespoons chopped parsley and serve with crusty bread.

Prawn and Goats' Cheese Salad

Serves 4

2 tablespoons walnut pieces

juice of 1 lime

1 tablespoon olive oil

1 fennel bulb, halved and sliced

1 red pepper, cored, deseeded
and sliced

2 pears, cored and sliced

200 g (7 oz) cooked peeled
king prawns

2 heads of chicory, leaves
separated

200 g (7 oz) firm goats' cheese,
cut into 4 slices

- Heat a nonstick frying pan over a medium-low heat and dry-fry the walnuts for 3–4 minutes, stirring frequently, until slightly golden. Set aside.

- Meanwhile, whisk together the lime juice and oil in a bowl.

- Toss together the fennel, red pepper, pears, prawns and chicory and place on a serving plate.

- Cook the goats' cheese under a preheated hot grill for 3–4 minutes until golden. Serve on the salad, drizzled with the dressing and sprinkled with the toasted walnuts.

2 Prawn and Cheese Soufflés

Melt 25 g (1 oz) butter in a small saucepan, then stir in 25 g (1 oz) plain flour. Cook for 1–2 minutes, then gradually whisk in 50 ml (2 fl oz) milk and cook, stirring, until thick and smooth. Add a pinch of cayenne pepper and season. Stir in 75 g (3 oz) grated Cheddar cheese and 3 egg yolks. Whisk 3 egg whites in a clean bowl until stiff. Stir 1 tablespoon of the egg white into the cheese sauce, then fold in the remainder. Place 100 g (3½ oz) cooked peeled prawns in 4 greased ramekins. Spoon the egg mixture into the ramekins and place on a baking sheet. Bake in a preheated oven, 190°C (350°F), Gas Mark 5, for 12–14 minutes. Serve immediately with a salad.

3 Prawn and Cheese Gratin

Toss 300 g (10 oz) raw peeled king prawns with the juice of 1 lime and a few drops of Tabasco sauce in a non-metallic bowl. Cover and leave to marinate in the refrigerator for 15 minutes. Meanwhile, heat 1 tablespoon olive oil in a frying pan, add 2 finely sliced red onions and cook for 2–3 minutes. Add 2 crushed garlic cloves and 2 deseeded and diced chillies and cook for a further 3–4 minutes. Divide the onion mixture between 4 gratin dishes. Drain the prawns and add to the onions. Pour over 150 ml (¼ pint) double cream and 150 ml (¼ pint) natural yogurt, then sprinkle with 75 g (3 oz) grated Cheddar cheese.

Cook under a preheated hot grill for 6–7 minutes until bubbling and the prawns turn pink. Serve with a crisp green salad.

20 Chunky Cod, Red Mullet and Prawn Stew

Serves 4

1 tablespoon olive oil
1 fennel bulb, quartered and
  thinly sliced
2 garlic cloves, thinly sliced
400 g (13 oz) can chopped
  tomatoes
pinch of saffron threads
900 ml (1½ pints) hot fish stock
250 g (8 oz) cod loin, cut into
  bite-sized pieces
200g (7 oz) cooked peeled
  king prawns
2 red mullet fillets, halved
  lengthways
50 g (2 oz) spinach leaves
crusty wholemeal bread, to serve

· Heat the oil in a large frying pan, add the fennel and garlic and cook for 4–5 minutes until softened. Stir in the tomatoes and saffron, then pour in the stock and bring to a simmer.

· Add the cod, prawns and red mullet and simmer for 6–8 minutes or until the fish is cooked through.

· Stir in the spinach until wilted, then serve immediately with crusty wholemeal bread.

10 Quick Cod, Red Mullet and Prawn Curry

Heat 1 tablespoon oil in a large frying pan or wok, add 1 chopped onion and 2 chopped garlic cloves and sauté for 1 minute. Stir in 2 tablespoons curry paste and a 400 ml (14 fl oz) can coconut milk and bring to a simmer. Add 200 g (7 oz) cod loin and 2 red mullet fillets, cut into bite-sized pieces, and 250 g (8 oz) cooked peeled king prawns. Simmer for 6–8 minutes until the fish is cooked through. Stir in 125 g (4 oz) spinach leaves and 2 tablespoons roughly chopped coriander. Season and serve with rice.

30 Cod, Red Mullet and Prawn Pie

Cook 750 g (1½ lb) peeled and chopped potatoes in a saucepan of boiling water for 10–12 minutes until tender. Meanwhile, place 350 g (11½ oz) red mullet and 250 g (8 oz) cod fillet in a frying pan with enough milk to cover and gently simmer for 5 minutes or until just cooked through. Drain, then skin and flake the fish and return to the pan with 100 g (3½ oz) peas, 100 g (3½ oz) cooked peeled prawns, 200 g (7 oz) crème fraîche and 2 tablespoons chopped chives and cook for a further 2–3 minutes. Drain the potatoes, then mash in the pan with 25 g (1 oz) butter and 2 tablespoons milk. Season well. Spoon the fish mixture into an ovenproof dish and top with the potato. Bake in a preheated oven, 200°C (400°F), Gas Mark 6, for 10 minutes until golden. Serve with steamed green vegetables.

QuickCook
Vegetarian Dishes

Recipes listed by cooking time

10 Quick Spinach and Mozzarella Pizzas

Serves 4

4 flour tortillas
1 tablespoon olive oil
625 g (1¼ lb) baby spinach leaves
400 g (13 oz) passata
100 g (3½ oz) roasted red pepper
  from a jar, cut into strips
6 spring onions, sliced
4 eggs
1 teaspoon dried oregano
225 g (7½ oz) mozzarella cheese,
  grated

- Place the tortillas on 2 large baking sheets and warm through in a preheated oven, 240°C (475°F), Gas Mark 9, for 2 minutes.

- Meanwhile, heat the oil in a large frying pan, add the spinach and cook briefly until wilted.

- Spread each tortilla with passata, then divide the spinach, red pepper and spring onions between them. Break an egg in the middle of each pizza, then sprinkle with the oregano and cheese.

- Return to the oven for a further 3–5 minutes until the edges are lightly browned and the cheese is melted.

20 Spinach and Mozzarella

Tagliatelle Cook 400 g (13 oz) tagliatelle in a large saucepan of boiling water for 9–10 minutes, or according to the pack instructions, until 'al dente'. Meanwhile, heat 1 tablespoon olive oil in a large frying pan, add 300 g (10 oz) baby spinach leaves and 2 crushed garlic cloves and cook until the spinach is wilted. Remove from the heat and stir in 100 g (3½ oz) roasted red pepper from a jar, cut into strips. Drain the pasta and toss with the spinach mixture and 200 g (7 oz) chopped mozzarella cheese. Serve sprinkled with chopped basil leaves and 2 tablespoons toasted pine nuts.

30 Spinach and Mozzarella

Roulade Whisk 3 egg whites and 1 teaspoon lemon juice in a clean bowl until stiff. In a separate bowl, mix together 1 teaspoon cornflour, 200 ml (7 fl oz) milk, 1 teaspoon Dijon mustard and 3 egg yolks and season with salt and pepper, then fold into the egg whites. Pour into a Swiss roll tin lined with greaseproof paper, spreading it out to the corners. Bake in a preheated oven, 180°C (350°F), Gas Mark 4, for 5–8 minutes until it springs back when pressed. Lift the roulade from the tin, then using the paper, roll it into a log and leave to cool for 5 minutes. Meanwhile,

heat 1 tablespoon olive oil in a frying pan, add 200 g (7 oz) baby spinach leaves and cook briefly until wilted, then stir in 2 chopped tomatoes and 100 g (3½ oz) sliced mozzarella cheese. Unroll the roulade, spread over the spinach filling, then re-roll. Serve with ready-made tomato sauce and a crisp green salad.

30 Red Pepper and Coconut Curry

Serves 4

1 teaspoon tamarind paste
1 teaspoon turmeric
½ teaspoon chilli powder
1 tablespoon mango juice
½ tablespoon coconut oil
1 teaspoon mustard seeds
2 teaspoons cumin seeds
2 garlic cloves, crushed
1 onion, sliced
1 teaspoon lazy ginger
800 ml (28 fl oz) coconut milk
175 g (6 oz) butternut squash,
   peeled, deseeded and chopped
1 potato, peeled and chopped
1 red pepper, cored, deseeded
   and chopped
1 parsnip, peeled and chopped
150 g (5 oz) cauliflower florets

To serve
2 tablespoons chopped coriander
2 tablespoons flaked almonds

- To make a spice paste, place the tamarind paste, powdered spices and mango juice in a mini food processor or small blender and blend together. Set aside.

- Heat the oil in a saucepan, add the mustard seeds and cumin seeds and cook until the mustard seeds begin to pop. Add the garlic, onion and ginger and cook for a further 3–4 minutes until softened.

- Add the spice paste and cook, stirring, for 1 minute, then pour in the coconut milk and bring to the boil. Add the vegetables and simmer for 20–22 minutes.

- Serve sprinkled with chopped coriander and flaked almonds.

1 Coconut-Crusted Tofu
Mix together 100 g (3½ oz) desiccated coconut, 1 tablespoon plain flour and 2 teaspoons cornflour on a plate. Cut 400 g (14 oz) tofu into thick slices and dip in a little milk and the desiccated coconut mixture. Heat 1 tablespoon olive oil in a frying pan, add the tofu and cook for 1–2 minutes on each side until slightly golden. Serve the salsa with the tofu and a rocket salad.

2 Roasted Red Peppers and Veg with Coconut Rice
Place 200 g (7 oz) peeled, deseeded and chopped butternut squash, 1 chopped red onion, cut into wedges, 2 cored, deseeded and chopped red peppers and 1 large sliced courgette in a roasting tin and toss with 1 tablespoon olive oil. Place in a preheated oven, 200°C (400°F), Gas Mark 6, for 18–19 minutes until tender. Meanwhile, place 200 g (7 oz) basmati rice, 360 ml (12 fl oz) half-fat coconut milk and 150 ml (¼ pint) water in a saucepan and season. Bring to a simmer, then cover and cook gently until all the liquid has been absorbed, adding a handful of defrosted frozen peas 3 minutes before the end of the cooking time. Stir in 4 chopped spring onions and 2 tablespoons chopped coriander. Serve with the roasted vegetables spooned over.

20 Butternut, Broccoli and Mushroom au Gratin

Serves 4

200 g (7 oz) purple sprouting broccoli, trimmed
300 g (10 oz) butternut squash, peeled, deseeded and chopped
200 g (7 oz) mushrooms, halved
60 g (2¼ oz) butter
2 tablespoons plain flour
400 ml (14 fl oz) milk
2 teaspoons wholegrain mustard
100 g (3½ oz) Cheddar cheese, grated

- Steam the vegetables in a steamer for 8–10 minutes until tender.

- Meanwhile, melt the butter in a small saucepan, then stir in the flour to make a roux. Cook for 1–2 minutes, then gradually whisk in the milk, and cook, stirring continuously, until the sauce is thick and smooth. Stir in the mustard and half the grated cheese.

- Transfer the vegetables to an ovenproof dish, pour over the sauce and sprinkle with the remaining cheese. Cook under a preheated hot grill for 5–6 minutes until bubbling and golden.

---

10 Cheesy Butternut Mash with Broccoli and Poached Eggs Cook 400 g (13 oz) peeled, deseeded and diced butternut squash and 150 g (5 oz) peeled and diced potatoes in a saucepan of boiling water for 8 minutes until tender. Meanwhile, bring a saucepan of water to a gentle simmer and stir with a large spoon to create a swirl. Break 2 eggs into the water and cook for 3 minutes. Remove with a slotted spoon and keep warm. Repeat with another 2 eggs. In a separate pan, steam 400 g (13 oz) broccoli florets until tender. Drain the squash and potatoes, then mash in the pan with 75 g (3 oz) grated Cheddar cheese. Serve topped with the broccoli and poached eggs, sprinkled with 2 tablespoons grated Parmesan cheese.

30 Butternut and Broccoli Soup with Mushroom Bruschetta Place 1 kg (2 lb) peeled, deseeded and chopped butternut squash and 1 head of broccoli, broken into large florets, in a roasting tin and sprinkle with 2 tablespoons olive oil. Place in a preheated oven, 220°C (425°F), Gas Mark 7, for 25 minutes until tender. Meanwhile, heat 1 tablespoon olive oil in a frying pan, add 150 g (5 oz) sliced chestnut mushrooms and fry for 7–8 minutes, then stir in 2 tablespoons chopped parsley. Toast 8 slices of baguette under a preheated hot grill for 2–3 minutes on each side. Rub one side of each slice with a garlic clove. Spoon the mushroom mix over the toasts and sprinkle with 2 tablespoons grated Parmesan cheese. Five minutes before the squash is cooked, heat 1 tablespoon olive oil in a saucepan, add 1 chopped onion and 1 teaspoon cumin seeds and cook until softened. Add the roasted vegetables and 1.5 litres (2½ pints) hot vegetable stock and bring to the boil. Remove from the heat and, using a hand-held blender, blend the soup until smooth. Serve with the mushroom bruschetta.

 # Moroccan Vegetable Stew

Serves 4

1 tablespoon olive oil
1 onion, chopped
2 garlic cloves, chopped
375 g (12 oz) sweet potatoes,
  peeled and chopped
175 g (6 oz) parsnips, chopped
275 g (9 oz) swede, chopped
2 large carrots, chopped
250 g (8 oz) Brussels sprouts
½ teaspoon ground cumin
1 teaspoon ground coriander
½ teaspoon turmeric
¼ teaspoon cayenne pepper
½ teaspoon ground cinnamon
400 g (13 oz) can tomatoes
400 ml (14 fl oz) vegetable stock
cooked couscous, to serve

- Heat the oil in a large, heavy-based saucepan, add the onion and garlic and fry for 2–3 minutes. Add all the vegetables, reduce the heat to low and cook, stirring occasionally, for 2–3 minutes without browning.

- Add the spices and mix well to coat all the vegetables, then pour in the tomatoes and vegetable stock. Bring to the boil, then reduce the heat and simmer, breaking up the tomatoes with a wooden spoon, for 20–22 minutes or until the vegetables are tender.

- Serve with couscous to soak up the juices.

1 — Moroccan Vegetable Soup

Heat 1 tablespoon oil in a saucepan, add 1 sliced red onion and 2 diced garlic cloves and cook for 1 minute. Stir in ½ teaspoon each of turmeric and ground cumin, ¼ teaspoon cayenne pepper and a pinch of ground cinnamon. Add 1 peeled, diced sweet potato, 2 cored, deseeded and sliced red peppers and ½ savoy cabbage, shredded. Pour in 1.2 litres (2 pints) vegetable stock and bring to the boil. Reduce the heat and simmer for 8 minutes. Blitz the soup briefly with a hand-held blender, then serve sprinkled with toasted flaked almonds.

2 — Moroccan Roasted Vegetables

Chop 1 large peeled carrot, 2 peeled sweet potatoes, 1 cored and deseeded red pepper, 1 cored and deseeded yellow pepper and 1 large peeled parsnip, then place in 2 roasting tins and sprinkle with 2 tablespoons cumin seeds and ½ teaspoon each of coriander seeds and turmeric. Pour over 2–3 tablespoons olive oil and toss together. Place in a preheated oven, 200°C (400°F), Gas Mark 6, for 15–17 minutes until all the vegetables are cooked and starting to char a little at the edges. Meanwhile, place 175 g (6 oz) couscous in a heatproof bowl and just cover with boiling water. Leave to stand for 12–15 minutes. Dry-fry 2 tablespoons cashew nuts in a nonstick frying pan for 3–4 minutes, stirring frequently, until golden. Fluff up the couscous with a fork. Stir in 2 tablespoons each of chopped coriander, chopped mint and chopped parsley, the juice of ½ lemon and 2 tablespoons extra virgin olive oil. Serve the vegetables spooned over the couscous, topped with the toasted cashews.

1 Broad Bean and Feta Tagliatelle

Serves 4

325 g (11 oz) tagliatelle
300 g (10 oz) fresh or frozen
  broad beans
2 tablespoons olive oil
6 spring onions, sliced
½ teaspoon dried chilli flakes
75 g (3 oz) watercress, roughly
  chopped
grated rind of 1 lemon
200 g (7 oz) feta cheese, crumbled
2 tablespoons toasted pine nuts

- Cook the pasta in a large saucepan of boiling water for 8–9 minutes, or according to the pack instructions, until 'al dente'. Add the broad beans 3 minutes before the end of the cooking time.

- Meanwhile, heat the oil in a large frying pan, add the spring onions and chilli flakes and cook for 2–3 minutes. Stir in the watercress and lemon rind.

- Drain the pasta and beans and add to the watercress mixture with the feta. Mix well.

- Serve sprinkled with the toasted pine nuts.

2 Broad Bean and Feta Salad

Place 250 g (8 oz) couscous in a large heatproof bowl and just cover with boiling water. Leave to stand for 10–12 minutes. Meanwhile, cook 300 g (10 oz) frozen broad beans in a saucepan of boiling water for 4–5 minutes until tender, then drain. Heat 1 tablespoon olive oil in a frying pan, add 125 g (4 oz) baby spinach leaves and cook briefly until wilted. Fluff up the couscous with a fork, then stir in the broad beans, spinach, 2 tablespoons chopped mint, 75 g (3 oz) sliced pitted black olives and 200 g (7 oz) crumbled feta cheese. Whisk together the juice of ½ lemon and 2 tablespoons olive oil in a small bowl, then drizzle over the salad and serve.

3 Broad Bean and Feta Mash

Cook 750 g (1½ lb) peeled and chopped potatoes in a saucepan of boiling water for 12–15 minutes until tender. Add 150 g (5 oz) defrosted and skinned broad beans and cook for a further minute, then drain. Meanwhile, heat a griddle pan until hot, add 12 trimmed asparagus spears and cook for 4–5 minutes, turning occasionally, until chargrilled. Keep warm. Bring a saucepan of water to a gentle simmer and stir with a large spoon to create a swirl. Break 2 eggs into the water and cook for 3 minutes. Remove with a slotted spoon and keep warm. Repeat with another 2 eggs. Drain the potatoes and beans, then mash in the pan with 100 g (3½ oz) crumbled feta cheese, 1 tablespoon natural yogurt or soured cream and salt and pepper until almost smooth. Serve topped with the asparagus and poached eggs.

HEA-VEGE-PYE

Cauliflower Cheese

Serves 4

1 large cauliflower, broken
into pieces
50 g (2 oz) butter
4 tablespoons plain flour
½ teaspoon English mustard
powder
500 ml (17 fl oz) milk
100 g (3½ oz) mature Cheddar
cheese, grated
2 tablespoons pumpkin seeds

- Cook the cauliflower in a large saucepan of boiling water for 5–6 minutes until tender.

- Meanwhile, melt the butter in a small saucepan, then stir in the flour and mustard powder to make a roux. Cook for 1–2 minutes, then gradually whisk in the milk and cook, stirring continuously, until the sauce is thick and smooth. Simmer for 1 minute, then stir in half the cheese.

- Drain the cauliflower and place in an ovenproof dish. Pour over the cheese sauce, then sprinkle with the pumpkin seeds and remaining cheese. Cook under a preheated hot grill for 2–3 minutes until bubbling and golden.

---

2 Cauliflower Cheese Soup

Melt 25 g (1 oz) butter in a saucepan, add 1 finely chopped onion and cook for 2–3 minutes. Add the florets of 1 large cauliflower, 1 peeled and chopped potato, 600 ml (1 pint) hot vegetable stock and 400 ml (14 fl oz) milk, season with salt and pepper and bring to the boil. Reduce the heat and simmer for 15–16 minutes until the vegetables are soft. Using a hand-held blender, blend the soup until smooth, adding a little more milk if needed. Sprinkle with 2 tablespoons grated mature Cheddar cheese.

3 Cauliflower and Macaroni Cheese

Cook 250 g (8 oz) macaroni in a saucepan of boiling water for 10–12 minutes, or according to the pack instructions, adding the florets of 1 large cauliflower 5 minutes before the end of the cooking time. Meanwhile, dry-fry 50 g (2 oz) walnut pieces in a nonstick frying pan for 3–4 minutes, stirring frequently, until slightly golden. Set aside. Melt 25 g (1 oz) butter in small saucepan, then stir in 2 tablespoons plain flour and 1 teaspoon English mustard powder to make a roux. Cook for 1–2 minutes, then gradually whisk in 450 ml (¾ pint) milk and cook, stirring continuously, until the sauce is thick and smooth. Stir in 50 g (2 oz) grated mature Cheddar cheese and season. Drain the macaroni and cauliflower, then return to the pan and stir in 4 chopped tomatoes and the toasted walnuts. Stir in the sauce, then transfer to an ovenproof dish and sprinkle over 50 g (2 oz) grated mature Cheddar and 2 tablespoons grated Parmesan cheese. Place in a preheated oven, 200°C (400°F), Gas Mark 6, for 10 minutes. Serve with a crisp green salad.

Roasted Peppers

Serves 4

2 red peppers, halved, cored
   and deseeded

2 yellow peppers, halved, cored
   and deseeded

1 small red onion, cut into
   8 wedges

2 runner beans, trimmed and
   cut into small batons

1 courgette, sliced

3 garlic cloves, sliced

2 tablespoons extra virgin olive oil

1 teaspoon cumin seeds

salt and pepper

100 g (3½ oz) feta or goats'
   cheese, to serve (optional)

- Place the pepper halves, cut side up, in a roasting tin and divide the vegetables and garlic between them.

- Sprinkle with the oil and cumin seeds and season with salt and pepper. Place in a preheated oven, 190°C (375°F), Gas Mark 5, for 25 minutes until tender. Sprinkle with feta or goats' cheese, to serve, if liked.

---

1 **Pepper and Courgette Salad**

Dry-fry 2 tablespoons pumpkin seeds in a nonstick frying pan for 2–3 minutes, stirring frequently, until golden brown. Set aside. Meanwhile, core, deseed and slice 2 red peppers and 1 yellow pepper. Place in a bowl with 100 g (3½ oz) halved cherry tomatoes, 50 g (2 oz) watercress and 2 grated courgettes. Toss with salad dressing and serve sprinkled with the toasted pumpkin seeds.

2 **Italian Fried Peppers**

Heat 2 tablespoons olive oil in a frying pan, add 1 sliced large onion and cook for 2–3 minutes until softened. Meanwhile, core, deseed and slice 2 red peppers, 2 yellow peppers and 2 orange peppers. Add 3 thinly sliced garlic cloves, the sliced peppers and 2 teaspoons dried oregano to the pan and cook for 3–4 minutes, then add 4 chopped tomatoes and 2 tablespoons torn basil leaves and cook for a further

12 minutes until the peppers are tender. Season with pepper and a squeeze of lemon juice.

Butter Bean and Mushroom Tagine

Serves 4

1 tablespoon olive oil
1 red onion, sliced
2 carrots, peeled and sliced
½ teaspoon mustard seeds
½ teaspoon cumin seeds
¼ teaspoon turmeric
800 ml (1 pint 8 fl oz) hot
   vegetable stock
1 tablespoon tomato purée
300 g (10 oz) mushrooms,
   chopped
400 g (13 oz) can butter beans,
   rinsed and drained
2 tablespoons chopped dill
salt and pepper
cooked rice, to serve

- Heat the oil in a saucepan, add the onion and sauté for 5–6 minutes until softened. Add the carrot and spices and cook for a further 2 minutes.

- Pour in the stock and stir in the tomato purée, then add the mushrooms and butter beans. Season with salt and pepper and add the dill, then simmer for 12–15 minutes.

- Serve with cooked rice.

1 **Warm Butter Bean and Mushroom Salad** Heat 2 tablespoons olive oil in a large frying pan, add 200 g (7 oz) sliced chestnut mushrooms and cook for 5–6 minutes until softened. Stir in a rinsed and drained 400 g (13 oz) can butter beans, 1 tablespoon balsamic vinegar, ½ teaspoon multigrain mustard and 1 teaspoon honey and stir well. Divide 150 g (5 oz) baby spinach leaves between 4 plates and spoon over the butter bean mixture. Serve sprinkled with 2 tablespoons chopped chives.

2 **Butter Bean and Mushroom Soup** Soak 15 g (½ oz) dried porcini in a small heatproof bowl of boiling water for 5 minutes. Meanwhile, heat 1 tablespoon olive oil in a frying pan, add 1 sliced onion and 2 crushed garlic cloves and cook for 4–5 minutes until softened. Add a rinsed and drained 400 g (13 oz) can butter beans and stir to coat with the oil. Drain and chop the porcini, then add to the pan with the soaking water, 175 g (6 oz) sliced chestnut mushrooms and 900 ml (1½ pints) hot vegetable stock. Bring to a simmer and cook for 12–14 minutes. Meanwhile, dry-fry 2 tablespoons pumpkin seeds in a nonstick frying pan for 2–3 minutes, stirring frequently, until lightly toasted. Using a hand-held blender, blend the soup until smooth, then stir in 3 tablespoons natural yogurt. Serve sprinkled with the toasted pumpkins seeds and a swirl of olive oil.

3❶ Cheesy Pesto Polenta

Serves 4

500 g (1 lb) butternut squash,
  peeled, deseeded and diced
3 tablespoons olive oil
1 large onion, chopped
½ teaspoon dried sage
750 ml (1¼ pints) water
175 g (6 oz) coarse polenta
75 g (3 oz) toasted pine nuts
40 g (1¾ oz) butter
2 tablespoons ready-made pesto
50 g (2 oz) Parmesan cheese,
  grated
salt and pepper
steamed Tenderstem broccoli,
  to serve

- Place the squash in a roasting tin and sprinkle over
  1 tablespoon of the oil. Place in a preheated oven, 200°C
  (400°F), Gas Mark 6, for 20–22 minutes until tender.

- Meanwhile, heat the remaining oil in a frying pan, add the
  onion and sage and season with salt and pepper, then cook
  over a low heat for 16–18 minutes, stirring occasionally,
  until soft and golden.

- In a separate pan, bring the water to the boil, then add the
  polenta in a steady stream, whisking continuously. Simmer
  over a low heat for 10–12 minutes until bubbling and cooked.

- Remove the squash from the oven, add the pine nuts and
  then roughly mash with a fork. Stir the butter, pesto,
  cheese, onions and mashed squash into the polenta, then
  serve with steamed broccoli.

1❶ Polenta Salad with Pesto Dressing

Heat 1 tablespoon oil in a pan, add
1 deseeded and diced chilli, 2 sliced
garlic cloves and 350 g (11½ oz)
sliced ready-made polenta and
cook for 3–4 minutes on each
side. Meanwhile, toss together
1 chopped romaine lettuce, 1 sliced
red onion, 2 deseeded and sliced
red peppers, 2 tablespoons olives,
3 sliced tomatoes and 2 sliced
avocados in a bowl. In a separate
bowl, whisk together 2 teaspoons
pesto, 3 tablespoons olive oil and
1 tablespoon white wine vinegar,
pour over the salad. Sprinkle the
polenta with 3 tablespoons grated
Parmesan and serve with the salad.

2❶ Polenta with Pesto Roasted Veg

Chop 1 cored and deseeded red
pepper, 1 cored and deseeded
yellow pepper, 2 courgettes,
2 red onions, 2 peeled carrots
and 125 g (4 oz) peeled sweet
potato, then place in 2 roasting
tins and sprinkle each with
1 tablespoon olive oil and season
with salt and pepper. Place
in a preheated oven, 200°C
(400°F), Gas Mark 6, for
16–18 minutes until roasted.
Meanwhile, heat 1 tablespoon
groundnut oil in a frying pan, add
2 tablespoons cumin seeds and
cook for 1 minute, then add
350 g (11½ oz) sliced ready-

made polenta and cook for
3–4 minutes on each side until
golden. Remove the vegetables
from the oven and stir in
2 tablespoons ready-made pesto.
Serve spooned over the polenta.

20  Asparagus and Pea Quinoa Risotto

Serves 4

275 g (9 oz) quinoa, rinsed
600 ml (1 pint) hot vegetable
  stock
200 g (7 oz) asparagus, chopped
200 g (7 oz) frozen peas
1 tablespoon chopped mint
3 tablespoons grated Parmesan
  cheese
pepper

- Place the quinoa and stock in a saucepan and bring to the boil, then reduce the heat and simmer for 12–15 minutes until the quinoa is cooked, adding the asparagus and peas about 2 minutes before the end of the cooking time.

- Drain the quinoa and vegetables, then return to the pan with the mint and 2 tablespoons of the cheese and season with pepper. Mix well.

- Serve sprinkled with the remaining Parmesan.

10 Warm Asparagus and Pea Rice Salad

Toss together 200 g (7 oz) asparagus tips and 1 tablespoon olive oil in a bowl, then cook in a preheated hot griddle pan for 2–3 minutes. Meanwhile, heat 200 g (7 oz) ready-cooked fresh white rice according to the pack instructions. Place the asparagus and rice in a large bowl. Cook 200 g (7 oz) frozen peas in a saucepan of boiling water for 1–2 minutes until tender, then drain and add to the rice with 2 tablespoons chopped mint, 1 tablespoon toasted pine nuts, 3 sliced spring onions, 1 tablespoon diced ready-to-eat dried apricots and salad dressing. Toss together and serve.

30 Asparagus and Pea Tart

Unroll a 375 g (12 oz) pack ready-rolled puff pastry and place on a baking sheet. Mix together 200 g (7 oz) cream cheese and 1 tablespoon Dijon mustard in a bowl, then spread over the pastry, leaving a 1.5 cm (¾ inch) border around the edge. Top with 300 g (10 oz) trimmed asparagus and 100 g (3½ oz) defrosted peas. Drizzle with 2 tablespoons olive oil, then season with pepper and sprinkle with 50 g (2 oz) grated Parmesan cheese. Place in a preheated oven, 200°C (400°F), Gas Mark 6, for 20–22 minutes. Serve with a crisp green salad.

 Greek Pitta Pockets

Serves 4

8 ready-cooked falafel
4 wholemeal pitta breads
¼ iceburg lettuce, shredded
½ cucumber, diced
12 cherry tomatoes, halved
10–12 mint leaves, torn
200 g (7 oz) ready-made
  hummus
4 tablespoons crumbled feta
  cheese

- Place the falafel on a baking sheet and bake in a preheated oven, 190°C (375°F), Gas Mark 5, for 10–12 minutes, or according to the pack instructions, turning once.

- Meanwhile, cook the pitta breads under a preheated medium grill for 4–5 minutes on each side until toasted, then split each down a long side to make a pocket.

- Toss together the lettuce, cucumber, tomatoes and mint in a bowl. Spoon the hummus into the pittas, then add the salad. Halve the falafel and place on the salad. Spoon over the feta to serve.

10 Greek Salad

Mix together 450 g (14½ oz) chopped tomatoes, 1 sliced red onion, 200 g (7 oz) crumbled feta cheese, ½ chopped cucumber, 20 pitted black olives, 1 tablespoon chopped parsley, 1 tablespoon chopped mint, 4 tablespoons olive oil and the juice of 1 lemon in a serving bowl. Serve with pitta breads.

30 Falafel with Greek Salsa

Put a rinsed and drained 400 g (13 oz) can chickpeas, 2 tablespoons tahini paste, 1 egg, 1 tablespoon grated lemon rind, the juice of ½ lemon, 1 teaspoon each of ground cumin and ground coriander and ½ teaspoon chilli powder in a food processor and pulse until almost smooth but still chunky. Transfer to a bowl and stir in 1 small chopped onion, 1 tablespoon chopped parsley, ½ tablespoon plain flour and ½ teaspoon baking powder. Using wet hands, shape into 2.5-cm (1-inch) patties, then cover and chill for 15 minutes. Meanwhile, mix together 4 chopped tomatoes, 1 tablespoon chopped parsley, 1 diced small red onion, 2 tablespoons chopped pitted black olives and 1 tablespoon chopped mint in a bowl. Season and stir in 2 tablespoons olive oil. Heat 5 mm (¼ inch) olive oil in a frying pan and cook the falafel for 3 minutes on each side until golden brown. Drain on kitchen paper, then serve with the salsa.

10 Fennel and Cumin Waldorf Salad

Serves 4

60 g (2¼ oz) walnut pieces
1 teaspoon ground cumin
300 g (10 oz) natural yogurt
100 g (3½ oz) green grapes,
  halved
1 small fennel bulb, thinly sliced
6 celery sticks, sliced diagonally
1 green apple, cored, quartered
  and thinly sliced
60 g (2¼ oz) sultanas

- Heat a nonstick frying pan over a medium-low heat and dry-fry the walnuts for 3–4 minutes, stirring frequently, until slightly golden. Leave to cool slightly.

- Mix together the cumin and yogurt in a large bowl. Add the remaining ingredients and the toasted walnuts and toss in the dressing until well coated.

- Serve immediately or cover and chill until required.

20 Fennel, Cumin and Butternut Soup

Heat 1 tablespoon olive oil in a saucepan, add 1 chopped onion and 1 teaspoon cumin seeds and cook for 1–2 minutes. Stir in 1 sliced fennel bulb, 2 peeled and diced carrots, 2 sliced celery sticks and 400 g (13 oz) peeled, deseeded and chopped butternut squash and cook for a further 3–4 minutes. Pour in 750 ml (1¼ pints) hot vegetable stock and bring to the boil, then reduce the heat and simmer for 12–14 minutes until the vegetables are tender. Using a hand-held blender, blend the soup until smooth. Season to taste. Serve with swirls of natural yogurt and crusty bread.

30 Cumin-Roasted Fennel and Veg

Toss together 2 fennel bulbs, cut into wedges, 2 large peeled and roughly chopped sweet potatoes, 1 red onion, cut into wedges, 2 peeled and chopped carrots, 2 cored, deseeded and chopped red peppers, 2 sliced courgettes, 2 tablespoons olive oil and 2 teaspoons cumin seeds in a roasting tin and season to taste. Place in a preheated oven, 200°C (400°F) Gas Mark 6, for 20–24 minutes until tender. Serve with baby spinach leaves, drizzled with balsamic glaze.

30 Mushroom, Tomato and Herb Pancakes

Serves 4

50 g (2 oz) buckwheat flour
50 g (2 oz) plain flour
1 egg
1 egg white
300 ml (½ pint) milk
2 tomatoes
100 g (3½ oz) unsalted butter
75 g (3 oz) chestnut mushrooms,
  sliced
1 tablespoon chopped parsley
1 tablespoon chopped basil
2 tablespoons grated Cheddar
  cheese, to serve

- Sift the flours into a large bowl, then make a well in the centre. Gradually whisk in the egg, egg white and milk until smooth. Leave to rest for 8 minutes.

- Meanwhile, place the tomatoes in a heatproof bowl and pour over boiling water to cover. Leave for 1–2 minutes, then drain, cut a cross at the stem end of each tomato and peel off the skins. Deseed and chop the flesh.

- Heat half the butter in a frying pan, add the tomatoes, mushrooms and herbs and cook for 5 minutes. Keep warm.

- Melt the remaining butter in 2 frying pans until foaming, then pour in enough of the batter to just cover the bases. Cook each pancake for about 3 minutes, then turn over and cook for a further 2 minutes. Remove from the pans and keep warm. Repeat with the remaining batter to make 8 pancakes.

- Divide the vegetable mixture between the pancakes and serve sprinkled with the cheese.

---

1 Mushroom, Tomato and Herb Toasts

Heat 1 tablespoon olive oil and 25 g (1 oz) butter in a frying pan, add 150 g (5 oz) sliced chestnut mushrooms and 1 crushed garlic clove and cook for 5–6 minutes until softened. Stir in 1 tablespoon chopped parsley and 12 quartered cherry tomatoes. Meanwhile, toast 4 slices of granary bread under a preheated hot grill for 2–3 minutes on each side. Spoon the mushrooms over the toasts and serve sprinkled with 1 tablespoon grated Parmesan cheese.

2 Tomato and Herb-Stuffed

Mushrooms Heat 1 tablespoon olive oil in a frying pan, add 1 chopped onion and 2 crushed garlic cloves and fry for 1–2 minutes, then remove from the pan with a slotted spoon. Trim the stalks from 4 portobello mushrooms, then add the cups to the pan, gill side up, and cook for 3–4 minutes. Mix together the onion mixture, 5 chopped tomatoes, 50 g (2 oz) grated Cheddar cheese, 1 tablespoon chopped parsley and 1 teaspoon thyme leaves in a bowl. Season well. Transfer the mushrooms to a baking sheet, spoon in the tomato mixture and sprinkle with 2 tablespoons grated Parmesan cheese. Place in a preheated oven, 180°C (350°F), Gas Mark 4, for 10–12 minutes. Serve with a herb salad tossed with a little olive oil and a squeeze of lemon juice.

Pea and Mint Pancakes

Serves 4

400 g (13 oz) fresh or frozen peas
1 large handful of mint leaves, chopped
50 g (2 oz) butter, melted
4 tablespoons plain flour
4 tablespoons natural yogurt
2 tablespoons grated Parmesan cheese
1 large egg
2 tablespoons groundnut oil
300 g (10 oz) Tenderstem broccoli, steamed
salt and pepper
4 large eggs, poached, to serve

- Cook the peas in a pan of boiling water for 2 minutes. Drain, then refresh under cold running water and drain again. Place in a food processor with the mint and blitz to form a rough texture. Add the butter, flour, yogurt, cheese and egg and season with salt and pepper. Blitz again to form a stiff paste.

- Heat the oil in a large frying pan, then drop 2 tablespoons of the pea mixture into the pan for each pancake. Smooth the tops and cook over a medium heat for 3–4 minutes. Turn the pancakes over and cook for a further 2 minutes. Remove from the pan and keep warm. Repeat with the remaining mixture to make about 12 pancakes.

- Heat a griddle pan until hot, add the broccoli and cook for 5–6 minutes, turning frequently, until slightly charred.

- Top the pancakes with the poached eggs and serve with the charred broccoli.

Pea and Mint Dip

Cook 500 g (1 lb) frozen peas in a saucepan of boiling water for 2 minutes. Drain, then refresh under cold running water and drain again. Place in a food processor with 125 g (4 oz) natural yogurt, a small handful of mint leaves and the juice of ½ lemon. Season well and blitz until nearly smooth. Serve with vegetable crudités and toasted pitta breads.

Pea and Mint Soufflés

Place 100 g (3½ oz) asparagus tips, 200 g (7 oz) frozen peas, 20 mint leaves and 150 ml (¼ pint) hot vegetable stock in a small saucepan and cook for 3–4 minutes until the vegetables are tender. Meanwhile, brush 4 ramekins with melted butter, then dust with 1 tablespoon grated Parmesan cheese. Transfer the pea mixture to a food processor or blender and blitz to a purée. Melt 20 g (¾ oz) butter in a small saucepan, then stir in 1–2 tablespoons plain flour to make a roux. Cook for 2–3 minutes, then gradually whisk in 200 ml (7 fl oz) milk and cook, stirring continuously, until the sauce is thick and smooth. Leave to cool, then put in a large bowl. Fold 4 egg yolks into the white sauce with the pea purée. Whisk 4 egg whites in a clean bowl until stiff, then gently fold into the pea mixture. Spoon into the ramekins, gently tap the dishes on the work surface and run a finger around the rims to ensure they will rise evenly. Place on a baking sheet and bake in a preheated oven, 200°C (400°F), Gas Mark 6, for 15 minutes until risen and golden. Serve immediately.

20 Linguine with Chickpea and Tomato Sauce

Serves 4

2 tablespoons olive oil

1 onion, chopped

2 garlic cloves, crushed

1 celery stick, sliced

400 g (13 oz) can chopped tomatoes

175 g (6 oz) baby spinach leaves

400 g (13 oz) can chickpeas, rinsed and drained

350 g (11½ oz) linguine

10 basil leaves, torn

50 g (2 oz) Parmesan cheese, grated, to serve

- Heat the oil in a large saucepan, add the onion, garlic and celery and cook for 3–4 minutes until softened. Add the tomatoes and bring to the boil, then reduce the heat and simmer for 10 minutes. Stir in the spinach and chickpeas and cook until the spinach is wilted.

- Meanwhile, cook the pasta in a saucepan of boiling water for 6–8 minutes, or according to the pack instructions, until 'al dente'. Drain, then add to the tomato sauce with the basil and toss together.

- Serve sprinkled with the Parmesan.

10 Chickpea, Tomato and Pasta Salad

Cook 300 g (10 oz) farfalle in a saucepan of boiling water for 7–8 minutes, or according to the pack instructions, until 'al dente'. Drain, then refresh under cold running water and drain again. Place in a serving bowl and toss together with a rinsed and drained 400 g (13 oz) can chickpeas, 1 diced red onion, 4 chopped tomatoes, 6 torn basil leaves, 50 g (2 oz) rocket leaves, 2 tablespoons Parmesan cheese shavings, 2 tablespoons olive oil and 1 tablespoon balsamic vinegar. Season to taste and serve.

30 Spaghetti with Roasted Tomato and Chickpea Sauce

Place 300 g (10 oz) halved tomatoes in a roasting tin, cut side up. Press 3 chopped garlic cloves into the tomatoes, then sprinkle with pepper and 2 tablespoons olive oil. Place in a preheated oven, 200°C (400°F), Gas Mark 6, for 25 minutes until very soft, adding 200 g (7 oz) canned chickpeas, rinsed and drained, 2–3 minutes before the end of the cooking time. Meanwhile, cook 350 g (11½ oz) spaghetti in a saucepan of boiling water for 8–9 minutes, or according to the pack instructions, until 'al dente'. Drain, then toss together with the tomatoes and chickpeas and 8 torn basil leaves. Serve sprinkled with 3 tablespoons toasted pine nuts.

 # Cheese and Spinach Quesadillas

Serves 4

275 g (9 oz) baby spinach leaves
8 flour tortillas
250 g (8 oz) goats' cheese
2 tablespoons sun-dried
    tomatoes, chopped
2 avocados, peeled, stoned
    and diced
1 red onion, thinly sliced
juice of 1 lime
2 tablespoons chopped coriander
salt and pepper

- Place the spinach in a pan with a small amount of water, then cover and cook until wilted. Drain and squeeze dry.

- Heat 2 nonstick frying pans, add 1 tortilla to each and crumble a quarter of the goats' cheese, followed by a quarter of the spinach and sun-dried tomatoes, over each tortilla. Season well.

- Place 1 tortilla on top of each and cook over a medium heat for 3–4 minutes until golden underneath. Gently turn the quesadillas over and cook for a further 3–4 minutes. Remove from the pans and keep warm. Repeat with the remaining 4 tortillas.

- Meanwhile, mix together the avocados, onion, lime juice and coriander in a bowl.

- Serve the quesadillas in wedges with the avocado salsa.

---

1 Cheese and Spinach Pancakes

Heat through 8 ready-made pancakes according to the pack instructions. Meanwhile, heat 2 tablespoons olive oil in a frying pan, add 150 g (5 oz) sliced chestnut mushrooms and cook for 3–4 minutes. Add 1 crushed garlic clove and 175 g (6 oz) baby spinach leaves and cook until wilted. Stir in 25 g (1 oz) grated Cheddar cheese. Divide the mixture between the pancakes, then roll them up and serve sprinkled with 50 g (2 oz) grated Cheddar and 1 tablespoon snipped chives.

3 Cheese and Spinach Muffins

Heat 25 g (1 oz) butter in a frying pan, add ½ diced onion and cook for 2–3 minutes until soft. Meanwhile, mix together 350 g (11½ oz) plain flour, 2½ teaspoons baking powder, 1 teaspoon paprika and 250 g (8 oz) grated Cheddar cheese in a large bowl. Beat together 200 ml (7 fl oz) milk and 1 egg in a jug, then pour into the dry ingredients and mix together until just combined – do not over-mix. Gently stir in the cooked onion and butter and 75 g (3 oz) roughly chopped

baby spinach leaves. Spoon into 12 paper muffin cases arranged in a muffin tin and cook in a preheated oven, 180°C (350°F), Gas Mark 4, for 25–26 minutes until golden.

Lentil, Mustard and Chickpea Soup

Serves 4

½ teaspoon coconut oil or olive oil
¼ teaspoon mustard seeds
½ teaspoon ground cumin
½ teaspoon turmeric
1 small onion, diced
1.5-cm (¾-inch) piece of fresh
   root ginger, finely chopped
1 garlic clove, finely chopped
100 g (3½ oz) red split lentils
250 g (8 oz) canned chickpeas,
   rinsed and drained
900 ml (1½ pints) hot vegetable
   stock
50 g (2 oz) baby spinach leaves
salt and pepper

- Heat the oil in a saucepan and add the dry spices. When the mustard seeds start to pop, add the onion, ginger and garlic and cook until the onion softens.

- Add the lentils and chickpeas and stir well to coat. Pour in the stock and bring to the boil, then reduce the heat and simmer for 14–16 minutes until the lentils are cooked.

- Stir in the spinach until wilted, then season to taste. Ladle the soup into bowls and serve.

---

1 **Lentil and Chickpea Salad with Warm Mustard Dressing** Heat 3 tablespoons olive oil in a large frying pan, add 1 deseeded and chopped red chilli, ½ teaspoon mustard seeds, 2 sliced garlic cloves and a 2.5-cm (1-inch) piece of root ginger, peeled and grated, and sauté for 2 minutes. Remove from the heat and stir in 1 small sliced red onion, a 400 g (13 oz) can lentils and a 400 g (13 oz) can chickpeas, rinsed and drained, the juice of ½ lemon and 2 tablespoons chopped sun-dried tomatoes. Stir together, pour into a serving bowl and toss with 60 g (2¼ oz) rocket leaves and 150 g (5 oz) crumbled feta cheese.

3 **Lentil, Chickpea, Chicken and Mustard Curry** Heat 1 tablespoon olive oil in a saucepan, add 450 g (14½ oz) chopped chicken breast fillets and cook until browned. Remove from the pan with a slotted spoon and set aside. Sauté 1 finely chopped onion, 1 teaspoon mustard seeds, 2 crushed garlic cloves and 1 diced red chilli in the pan for 2–3 minutes. Stir in ½ teaspoon turmeric, ½ teaspoon paprika, 1 teaspoon ground cumin, ½ teaspoon garam masala and 1 teaspoon ground coriander and cook for 1 minute. Stir in a 400 g (13 oz) can chopped tomatoes and 200 ml (7 fl oz) hot vegetable stock, then return the chicken to the pan. Simmer for 12–15 minutes. Stir in a rinsed and drained 400 g (13 oz) can lentils and a rinsed and drained 400 g (13 oz) can chickpeas and simmer for a further 5 minutes until cooked through and piping hot. Stir in 2 tablespoons chopped coriander and serve with cooked basmati rice.

Carrot and Cashew Rice

Serves 4

1 tablespoon olive oil
1 red onion, chopped
2 garlic cloves, sliced
2 teaspoons mustard seeds
1 teaspoon cumin seeds
1 teaspoon coriander seeds
1 teaspoon ground coriander
1 teaspoon turmeric
250 g (8 oz) carrots, peeled
  and grated
250 g (8 oz) basmati rice
500 ml (17 fl oz) hot vegetable
  stock
50 g (2 oz) cashew nuts
2 tablespoons chopped coriander
salt and pepper

- Heat the oil in a saucepan, add the onion and garlic and cook for 2–3 minutes. Stir in the spices and cook for 1 minute, then stir in the carrots and rice.

- Pour in the stock and season with salt and pepper. Bring to the boil, then cover tightly and cook over a medium heat for 15 minutes. Remove from the heat and leave to stand for 10 minutes.

- Meanwhile, heat a nonstick frying pan over a medium-low heat and dry-fry the cashews for 3–4 minutes, stirring frequently, until golden and toasted.

- Fluff up the rice with a fork, then stir in the toasted cashews and coriander.

10 Carrot and Cashew Slaw

Dry-fry 150 g (5 oz) cashew nuts as above. Mix together 5 peeled and grated carrots, 1 shredded small white cabbage and 1 thinly sliced small red onion in a serving bowl, then toss in the cashews. Heat 1 tablespoon olive oil in a frying pan, add 2 teaspoons mustard seeds and 1 tablespoon cumin seeds and cook until the mustard seeds start to pop. Stir in 2 tablespoons white wine vinegar and season. Pour over the carrot mixture and toss together with 2 tablespoons coriander leaves

20 Carrot and Cashew Curry

Heat 1 tablespoon coconut oil in a wok or large frying pan, add 1 chopped onion and stir-fry for 1 minute. Stir in 2 tablespoons peeled and grated fresh root ginger, 2 crushed garlic cloves, 2 teaspoons garam masala, ½ teaspoon chilli powder and 1 teaspoon turmeric. Add 700 g (1½ lb) carrots, cut into batons, 200 g (7 oz) cashew nuts, 200 g (7 oz) canned chopped tomatoes and 50 ml (2 fl oz) hot vegetable stock. Bring to a simmer, then cook, covered, for 15–16 minutes until the carrots are soft. Serve with cooked basmati rice.

Chilli and Sprouting Broccoli Pasta with Poached Eggs

Serves 4

300 g (10 oz) linguine

250 g (8 oz) purple sprouting broccoli

4 eggs

2 tablespoons olive oil

6 spring onions, sliced

1 teaspoon dried chilli flakes

12 cherry tomatoes, halved

· Cook the pasta in a large saucepan of boiling water for 6 minutes. Add the broccoli and cook for a further 4–5 minutes until the pasta is 'al dente' and the broccoli is tender.

· Meanwhile, bring a saucepan of water to a gentle simmer and stir with a large spoon to create a swirl. Break 2 of the eggs into the water and cook for 3 minutes. Remove with a slotted spoon and keep warm. Repeat with the remaining eggs.

· Drain the pasta and broccoli and keep warm. Heat the oil in the pasta pan, add the spring onions, chilli flakes and tomatoes and fry, stirring, for 2–3 minutes. Return the pasta and broccoli to the pan and toss well to coat with the chilli oil.

· Serve the pasta topped with the poached eggs.

---

10 Chillied Sprouting Broccoli and Haloumi Cook 550 g (1 lb 3 oz) purple sprouting broccoli in boiling water for 3 minutes. Drain, then toss with 1 tablespoon olive oil, ½ teaspoon dried chilli flakes and ½ tablespoon black pepper. Cook in a preheated hot griddle pan for 2 minutes on each side. Meanwhile, cook 200 g (7 oz) sliced haloumi in a nonstick frying pan for 2 minutes on each side. Whisk together the juice of ½ lemon, 2 tablespoons olive oil, 2 tablespoons tahini and 1 tablespoon white wine vinegar in a small bowl. Place the broccoli and haloumi on a large serving plate, sprinkle with 3 tablespoons toasted chopped walnuts and drizzle with the dressing.

30 Chilli, Sprouting Broccoli and Red Pepper Noodles Halve, core and deseed 3 red peppers and cook under a preheated hot grill, skin side up, for 10–12 minutes until blackened. Place in a bowl, cover with clingfilm and leave to cool for 5 minutes. Meanwhile, cook 300 g (10 oz) purple sprouting broccoli in a saucepan of boiling water for 5–6 minutes until tender, then drain, refresh under cold running water and drain again. Cut in half lengthways. Cook 100 g (3½ oz) ramen noodles according to the pack instructions, adding 100 g (3½ oz) soya beans 2 minutes before the end of the cooking time. Drain and place in a large bowl with the broccoli. Mix together 1 tablespoon soy sauce, 1 teaspoon dried chilli flakes, 2 teaspoons sesame oil, ½ teaspoon peeled and grated fresh root ginger, 2 sliced spring onions and 2 tablespoons olive oil in a bowl. Peel the skin from the red peppers, then cut into strips. Add to the broccoli and toss with the dressing and 150 g (5 oz) crumbled feta cheese.

HEA-VEGE-GOZ

3 ◑ Simple Baked Leeks and Sweet Potatoes

Serves 4

4 small sweet potatoes
4 teaspoons sea salt
4 leeks, trimmed, halved and sliced
150 ml (¼ pint) white wine
2 tablespoons extra virgin olive oil
75 g (3 oz) Parmesan cheese, grated
2 garlic cloves, crushed
40 g (1¾ oz) pine nuts
pepper

- Prick the sweet potatoes with a knife or fork, then wash and rub with the salt. Bake in a preheated oven, 200°C (400°F), Gas Mark 6, for 25 minutes until tender.

- Meanwhile, place the leeks in a shallow ovenproof dish and sprinkle with the wine and oil. Season with pepper. Mix together the cheese, garlic and pine nuts in a bowl, then sprinkle over the leeks.

- Cover with foil and place in the oven for 15 minutes, then remove the foil and cook for a further 12–13 minutes.

- Halve the sweet potatoes and serve with the leeks.

1 ◔ Roasted Baby Leeks and Sweet Potatoes

Blanch 16 trimmed baby leeks and 250 g (8 oz) peeled and finely diced sweet potatoes in a saucepan of boiling water for 2 minutes, then drain and place in a roasting tin. Toss together with 2 tablespoons olive oil and bake in a preheated oven, 200°C (400°F), Gas Mark 6, for 8 minutes until tender. Meanwhile, mix together 4 chopped tomatoes, 2 tablespoons olive oil, 2 tablespoons chopped sun-dried tomatoes, 1 tablespoon red wine vinegar, 4 sliced spring onions and 1 tablespoon chopped parsley in a bowl. Spoon over the leeks and sweet potatoes, then sprinkle with 2 tablespoons Parmesan cheese shavings.

2 ◔ Leek and Sweet Potato Soup

Heat 2 tablespoons olive oil in a large saucepan, add 1 chopped onion and 2 trimmed and chopped leeks and sauté for 2–3 minutes. Add 225 g (7½ oz) peeled and chopped sweet potatoes and 1.2 litres (2 pints) hot vegetable stock and bring to the boil. Season, then reduce the heat and simmer for 15–16 minutes until the vegetables are tender. Using a hand-held blender, blend the soup until smooth, then stir in 2–3 tablespoons natural yogurt. Serve with a sprinkling of chopped parsley.

Mushroom and Tofu Stew

Serves 4

1 tablespoon olive oil

1 onion, sliced

500 g (1 lb) chestnut mushrooms, quartered

350 g (11½ oz) sweet potatoes, peeled and chopped

½ tablespoon pomegranate molasses or balsamic syrup

1 tablespoon wholemeal flour

500 ml (17 fl oz) hot vegetable stock

1 tablespoon dark muscovado sugar

dash of Worcestershire sauce

200 g (7 oz) tofu, cubed

steamed Tenderstem broccoli, to serve

- Heat the oil in a large saucepan or flameproof casserole dish, add the onion and cook for 1–2 minutes until it starts to soften. Add the mushrooms and cook for a further 1–2 minutes, stirring occasionally.

- Add the sweet potatoes, molasses or syrup and flour and stir well. Slowly pour in the stock, stirring continuously. Add the sugar and Worcestershire sauce and stir again until well mixed.

- Bring to a simmer, cover and cook for 15 minutes until the sweet potatoes are tender. Add the tofu 5 minutes before the end of the cooking time.

- Serve with steamed Tenderstem broccoli.

Mushroom and Tofu Stir-Fry

Heat 1 tablespoon coconut oil in a wok or large frying pan, add 2 sliced red onions, 1 tablespoon mustard seeds and 2 chopped garlic cloves and stir-fry for 1–2 minutes. Add 500 g (1 lb) sliced chestnut mushrooms and stir-fry for 2–3 minutes, then add 1 cored, deseeded and sliced red pepper, ½ shredded Chinese cabbage and 150 g (5 oz) cubed tofu and stir-fry for a further 4–5 minutes. Stir in 2 teaspoons soy sauce. Serve sprinkled with 2 tablespoons toasted sesame seeds.

Mushroom and Tofu Thai Curry

Heat 1 tablespoon coconut oil in a wok or large frying pan, add 1 red onion, 2 kaffir lime leaves, 1 tablespoon mustard seeds and 2 chopped garlic cloves and stir-fry for 1–2 minutes. Stir in 2 teaspoons Thai red chilli paste. Pour in a 400 ml (14 fl oz) can coconut milk and simmer for 3–4 minutes, stirring occasionally, then add 2 cored, deseeded and chopped red peppers, 150 g (5 oz) peeled and chopped sweet potatoes, 400 g (13 oz) sliced chestnut mushrooms and 2 chopped tomatoes and cook for 18–20 minutes until the sweet potatoes are tender. Stir in 2 tablespoons coriander leaves and serve with cooked basmati rice.

Cheesy Spinach-Stuffed Mushrooms

Serves 4

8 portobello mushrooms, stalks removed
4 tablespoons olive oil
6 spring onions, sliced
400 g (13 oz) baby spinach leaves
225 g (7½ oz) ready-cooked fresh basmati rice
100 g (3½ oz) Manchego cheese, grated
salt and pepper

- Place the mushrooms, gill side up, in a large roasting tin, drizzle with 1 tablespoon of the oil and cook in a preheated oven, 200°C (400°F), Gas Mark 6, for 6–8 minutes.

- Meanwhile, heat the remaining oil in a large frying pan, add the spring onions and sauté for 3–4 minutes. Gradually add the spinach, stirring until wilted. Add the rice and half the cheese and season to taste, then mix well.

- Remove the mushrooms from the oven and divide the spinach mixture between the caps. Sprinkle with the remaining cheese and cook for a further 8–10 minutes.

1 ⏲ **Spinach, Mushrooms and Cheese on Toast** Heat 1 tablespoon olive oil in a frying pan, add 4 spring onions and sauté for 1 minute, then add 200 g (7 oz) sliced chestnut mushrooms and cook for 5–6 minutes. Add 100 g (3½ oz) baby spinach leaves, stirring until wilted. Meanwhile, toast 4 slices of granary bread under a preheated hot grill for 2–3 minutes on each side. Stir 150 g (5 oz) crumbled Stilton cheese into the mushroom mixture and spoon over the toasts to serve.

3 ⏲ **Spinach, Mushroom and Feta-Stuffed Peppers** Place 4 halved, cored and deseeded peppers in a roasting tin, cut side up. Heat 1 tablespoon olive oil in a frying pan, add 1 large chopped red onion and 1 teaspoon cumin seeds and cook for 2–3 minutes. Add 6 sliced chestnut mushrooms and cook for a further 2 minutes, then add 350 g (11½ oz) baby spinach leaves, cover and cook for 2–3 minutes until the spinach is wilted. Remove from the heat and add 25 g (1 oz) chopped walnuts, 25 g (1 oz) pumpkin seeds and 200 g (7 oz) crumbled feta cheese. Season well, then spoon the mixture into the peppers. Place in a preheated oven, 200°C (400°F), Gas Mark 6, for 20–22 minutes until the peppers are tender. Meanwhile, cook 500 g (1 lb) peeled, deseeded and chopped butternut squash and 200 g (7 oz) peeled and chopped potatoes in a saucepan of boiling water for 12–15 minutes until tender. Drain, then mash in the pan with 1 tablespoon natural yogurt and 1 teaspoon chopped thyme leaves. Serve the peppers with the mash.

Falafel with Spicy Sauce

Serves 4

400 g (13 oz) can chickpeas,
  rinsed and drained
1 onion, finely diced
2 garlic cloves, chopped
3 tablespoons chopped parsley
1 teaspoon ground coriander
1 teaspoon ground cumin
2 tablespoons plain flour
2–3 tablespoons vegetable oil
salt and pepper
½ iceburg lettuce, shredded,
  to serve

For the spicy sauce

100 g (3½ oz) tomato purée
½–1 teaspoon harissa paste,
  to taste
2 garlic cloves, crushed
1 teaspoon lemon juice
50 ml (2 fl oz) water
1 tablespoon chopped parsley

- To make the sauce, place all the ingredients in a small saucepan and simmer for 10 minutes.

- Meanwhile, place all the falafel ingredients except the oil in a large bowl and mash together with a fork. Alternatively, place the ingredients in a food processor and blitz until smooth. Using wet hands, shape the mixture into small balls and flatten slightly.

- Heat the vegetable oil in a frying pan and cook the falafel for 5–7 minutes until golden.

- Serve on the lettuce with the spicy sauce.

2 Falafel and Tabbouleh Salad

Make the falafel as above. Meanwhile, place 250 g (8 oz) couscous in a heatproof bowl and just cover with boiling water. Leave to stand for 10 minutes. Fluff up the couscous with a fork, then stir in 2 tablespoons each of chopped mint, chopped parsley and chopped chives, 3 diced tomatoes and ½ diced cucumber. Serve with the falafel and dollops of ready-made hummus.

3 Falafel and Haloumi Burgers

Place 625 g (1¼ lb) canned chickpeas, rinsed and drained, 2 teaspoons ground cumin, 1 teaspoon ground coriander, 2 deseeded and diced green chillies, 2 chopped garlic cloves, 6 chopped spring onions, ½ teaspoon salt and 2 tablespoons plain flour in a food processor and whizz until coarsely blended. Transfer to a bowl and stir in 200 g (7 oz) diced haloumi cheese. Using wet hands, shape into 4 burgers, then cover and chill for 15 minutes. Heat 1 tablespoon olive oil in a frying pan, add the burgers and cook for 3–4 minutes on each side until golden. Meanwhile, toast 4 burger buns under a preheated medium grill for 3–4 minutes on each side. Top the bases with 2 tablespoons shredded iceburg lettuce. Place a burger on top, then 3 sliced tomatoes. Top with the lids and serve immediately.

Crunchy Pesto Broccoli with Poached Eggs

Serves 4

625 g (1¼ lb) broccoli florets
300 g (10 oz) sugar snap peas
4 eggs
75 g (3 oz) sun-dried tomatoes,
  chopped
pepper
Parmesan cheese shavings,
  to serve

For the pesto

10 g (⅓ oz) basil leaves
5 g (¼ oz) toasted pine nuts
5 g (¼ oz) Parmesan cheese,
  grated
1 small garlic clove, crushed
15–20 ml (½–¾ fl oz) olive oil

- To make the pesto, place the basil and pine nuts in a food processor and blitz until broken down. Add the cheese and garlic and blitz briefly. With the motor still running, slowly pour in the oil through the feed tube until combined.

- Cook the broccoli and sugar snap peas in a large saucepan of boiling water for 7–8 minutes until 'al dente'.

- Meanwhile, bring a saucepan of water to a gentle simmer and stir with a large spoon to create a swirl. Break 2 of the eggs into the water and cook for 3 minutes. Remove with a slotted spoon and keep warm. Repeat with the remaining eggs.

- Drain the vegetables, then return to the pan and add 1½ tablespoons of the pesto (store any remaining pesto in an airtight container in the refrigerator) and the sun-dried tomatoes. Gently toss together until well coated.

- Serve topped with the poached eggs and Parmesan shavings and sprinkled with pepper.

Broccoli Pesto Pasta

Cook 400 g (13 oz) green tagliatelle in a saucepan of boiling water for 8–9 minutes, or according to the pack instructions, until 'al dente', adding 150 g (5 oz) broccoli florets 3 minutes before the end of the cooking time. Drain, then return to the pan with 4 tablespoons ready-made pesto, 4 chopped spring onions and 100 g (3½ oz) chopped goats' cheese. Toss together and serve immediately.

Pesto and Broccoli Potato Cakes

Cook 1 kg (2 lb) peeled and chopped potatoes in a saucepan of boiling water for 12–15 minutes until tender, adding 100 g (3½ oz) broccoli florets 2 minutes before the end of the cooking time. Drain, then mash in the pan with 2 tablespoons crème fraîche. Stir in 1 tablespoon ready-made pesto and 4 sliced spring onions and season well. Using wet hands, shape into 4 patties. Heat 2 tablespoons olive oil in a frying pan, add the potato cakes and cook for 2–3 minutes on each side until golden. Meanwhile, poach 4 eggs as above. Serve the potato cakes topped with the poached eggs.

HEA-VEGE-CEF

QuickCook
Cakes and Desserts

Recipes listed by cooking time

30

20

10

3⦿ Lemon and Raisin Scones

Makes 12

30 g (1 oz) raisins
juice of ½ lemon
grated rind of 2 lemons
450 g (14½ oz) self-raising
  flour, sifted
75 g (3 oz) chilled butter, diced
3 tablespoons caster sugar
300 ml (½ pint) milk

To serve

2 tablespoons Greek yogurt
2 tablespoons lemon curd

- Place the raisins in a small bowl and pour over the lemon juice. Leave to stand for 10 minutes.

- Meanwhile, place the lemon rind and flour in a large bowl, add the butter and rub in with the fingertips until the mixture resembles fine breadcrumbs. Drain the raisins, then stir in with the sugar. Using a palette knife, gradually mix in the milk to form a dough – do not over-mix or knead.

- Turn the dough out on to a floured surface and press out lightly to about 2 cm (¾ inch) thick, then cut out 12 rounds using a 4–5-cm (1½–2-inch) plain biscuit cutter, using the trimmings as necessary.

- Place on a baking sheet and bake in a preheated oven, 200°C (400°F), Gas Mark 6, for 12–15 minutes until risen and slightly coloured. Transfer to a wire rack to cool.

- Serve with Greek yogurt and lemon curd.

1⦿ Lemon Mousse
Whisk together 300 ml (½ pint) double cream, the grated rind of 1 lemon and 60 g (2¼ oz) caster sugar in a bowl until the mixture starts to thicken. Add the juice of 1 lemon and whisk again until thickened. Whisk 2 egg whites in a clean bowl until they form soft peaks, then gently fold into the cream mixture. Spoon into 4 glasses and chill for a few minutes before serving.

2⦿ Lemon and Cardamom Biscuits
Beat together 225 g (7½ oz) softened unsalted butter, 150 g (5 oz) caster sugar and the grated rind of 1 lemon until light and fluffy. Beat in 250 g (8 oz) plain flour, 100 g (3½ oz) ground almonds and 2 teaspoons ground cardamom to form a stiff dough. Roll the dough into 24 balls and place, well spaced apart, on a baking sheet lined with greaseproof paper. Press each ball to flatten slightly, then bake in a preheated oven, 190°C (375°F), Gas Mark 5, for 12–14 minutes until golden. Leave to cool on the baking sheet for 2 minutes, then transfer to a wire rack to cool completely.

Oat-Topped Pear and Ginger Pudding

Serves 4–6

8 ripe pears, peeled, cored and chopped
4–5 knobs of stem ginger, diced
3 tablespoons stem ginger syrup
50 g (2 oz) coconut oil
45 g (1¾ oz) molasses
25 g (1 oz) light muscovado sugar
120 g (4 oz) rolled oats
25 g (1 oz) pumpkin seeds
10 g (⅓ oz) sesame seeds

- Place the pears in a shallow ovenproof dish, then sprinkle over the stem ginger. Pour over the stem ginger syrup.

- Heat the oil, molasses and sugar in a saucepan over a gentle heat, stirring until the sugar is dissolved. Add the remaining ingredients and mix well. Spoon the mixture over the pears.

- Bake in a preheated oven, 190°C (375°F), Gas Mark 5, for 15–17 minutes until golden.

---

1 Caramelized Pears with Ginger Yogurt

Heat 25 g (1 oz) butter in a frying pan, add 4 peeled, cored and sliced pears and cook for 3–4 minutes on each side. Meanwhile, stir 4 diced knobs of stem ginger and 2 tablespoons stem ginger syrup into 200 ml (7 fl oz) thick natural yogurt. Serve the pears topped with dollops of the ginger yogurt and a sprinkling of flaked almonds.

3 Ginger Poached Pears

Place 750 g (1½ lb) caster sugar, 1 cinnamon stick, 2 strips of lemon rind, 1 star anise, 1 vanilla pod, 5 cloves and a 2.5-cm (1-inch) piece of fresh root ginger, peeled and sliced, in a large saucepan. Half-fill the pan with water, then bring to the boil. Add 4 peeled ripe pears, cover and gently poach for about 20 minutes until tender.

Turn off the heat and leave to cool slightly. Serve the pears with a little of the syrup, sprinkled with 1 chopped knob of stem ginger and scoops of vanilla ice cream, if liked.

Berry Eton Mess

Serves 4

50 g (2 oz) meringue nests,
broken into chunks
350 g (11½ oz) mixed berries,
such as strawberries,
raspberries, blueberries and
blackberries, defrosted if frozen
300 g (10 oz) natural bio yogurt
2 knobs of stem ginger, diced

- Place the meringues in a large bowl and add the berries and yogurt. Mix very gently so the meringue pieces do not break up too much.

- Divide between 4 glasses or bowls and sprinkle with the stem ginger.

Berry and Rhubarb Fool

Place 400 g (13 oz) trimmed and chopped rhubarb, 200 g (7 oz) hulled and halved strawberries, the juice of 1 orange and 2 tablespoons sugar in a saucepan and bring to a simmer, then cook gently for 8–10 minutes. Transfer to a bowl and chill for 6 minutes. Meanwhile, finely chop a small handful of mint leaves and stir into 400 ml (14 fl oz) thick natural yogurt. Layer the fruit and yogurt in 4 glasses and serve each with a light sweet biscuit, if liked.

Berry Muffins

Sift 200 g (7 oz) self-raising flour into a large bowl and stir in 225 g (7½ oz) caster sugar. Beat together the grated rind of 1 orange, 250 ml (8 fl oz) thick natural yogurt, 50 g (2 oz) melted butter and 1 beaten egg in a jug, then pour into the dry ingredients and mix together – do not over-mix. Gently stir in 150 g (5 oz) mixed berries and the segments from 1 orange until just combined. Spoon into 12 paper muffin cases arranged in a muffin tin and bake in a preheated oven, 190°C (375°F), Gas Mark 5, for 20–25 minutes until golden and firm to the touch. Transfer to a wire rack to cool or serve warm.

30 Cocoa, Orange and Pecan Flapjack

Makes 9–12

100 g (3½ oz) coconut oil, plus extra for greasing
90 g (3¼ oz) blackstrap molasses
20 g (¾ oz) dark muscovado sugar
25 g (1 oz) agave syrup
250 g (8 oz) rolled oats
50 g (2 oz) pecan nuts, roughly chopped
50 g (2 oz) cocoa nibs
grated rind of 1 orange

• Heat the oil, molasses, sugar and agave syrup in a large saucepan over a gentle heat, stirring until the sugar is dissolved. Add the remaining ingredients and mix well.

• Pour into a greased 18 cm (7 inch) square baking tin and level the surface. Bake in a preheated oven, 180° (350°F), Gas Mark 4, for 18–20 minutes.

• Cool in the tin for 2 minutes, then cut into squares. Leave to cool completely in the tin.

1 Cocoa, Orange and Pecan Muesli

Dry-fry 50 g (2 oz) pecan nuts in a nonstick frying pan for 3–4 minutes, stirring frequently, until toasted. Leave to cool, then mix together with 250 g (8 oz) rolled oats, 50 g (2 oz) cocoa nibs, 50 g (2 oz) diced ready-to-eat dried apricots and the grated rind of 2 oranges. Soak for a few minutes in the juice of 2 oranges, then serve with fresh fruit and natural yogurt.

2 Cocoa, Orange and Pecan Scones

Toast 25 g (1 oz) pecan nuts (see left), then chop. Set aside. Sift together 225 g (7½ oz) self-raising flour and a pinch of salt in a large bowl. Add 75 g (3 oz) diced chilled unsalted butter and rub in with the fingertips until the mixture resembles fine breadcrumbs. Stir in the pecans, 40 g (1¾ oz) caster sugar, the grated rind of 1 orange, and 25 g (1 oz) cocoa nibs. Beat together 1 egg and 2 tablespoons buttermilk in a jug, then add to the dry ingredients and mix with a palette knife to a soft dough. Roll or press out on a floured surface to 2.5-cm (1-inch) thick, then cut out rounds using a 5 cm (2 inch) plain biscuit cutter or glass. Place on a baking sheet and bake in a preheated oven, 220°C (425°F), Gas Mark 7, for 10–12 minutes until risen. Transfer to a wire rack to cool.

20  Sweet Semolina with Cardamom Poached Apricots

Serves 4

½ vanilla pod, split lengthways
2 tablespoons honey
6 cardamom pods, lightly crushed
200 ml (7 fl oz) water
4 apricots, halved and stoned
600 ml (1 pint) milk
50 g (2 oz) semolina
25 g (1 oz) caster sugar
pinch of nutmeg
1 tablespoon pistachio nuts,
    chopped

- Scrape the seeds from the vanilla pod and add the seeds and pod to a saucepan with the honey, cardamom pods and measurement water. Bring to the boil, stirring occasionally, until the honey dissolves.

- Add the apricots and simmer for 2–5 minutes until just tender. Remove the apricots with a slotted spoon.

- Boil the remaining syrup over a high heat for 6–8 minutes until reduced by about half, then strain.

- Meanwhile, bring the milk to a boil in a separate saucepan, then slowly pour in the semolina and sugar, stirring continuously. Simmer and stir for 8–10 minutes until thickened and cooked. Add the nutmeg.

- Spoon the semolina into 4 small bowls and add the apricots. Pour over the syrup and serve sprinkled with the pistachios.

---

10 **Cardamom Rice Pudding with Apricots** Place 75 g (3 oz) flaked rice, 750 ml (1¼ pints) semi-skimmed milk and 4 lightly crushed cardamom pods in a saucepan and bring to the boil, stirring occasionally. Reduce the heat and simmer, stirring occasionally, for 7 minutes. Stir in 4–5 teaspoons caster sugar. Serve the rice pudding topped with a 400 g (13 oz) can apricots in syrup.

30 **Apricot Tarts with Cardamom Yogurt** Unroll a 375 g (12 oz) pack ready-rolled puff pastry and cut into 4 rectangles. Place on a baking sheet and top each one with 1 tablespoon ground almonds. Lay 2–3 halved and stoned apricots on top and dust with 2 tablespoons icing sugar. Bake in a preheated oven, 220°C (425°F), Gas Mark 7, for 20–25 minutes until golden. Meanwhile, remove the seeds from 3–4 cardamom pods and crush using a pestle and mortar, then mix together with 200 g (7 oz) Greek yogurt in a bowl. Serve the apricots tarts with the yogurt, sprinkled with a few chopped pistachio nuts and a drizzle of honey.

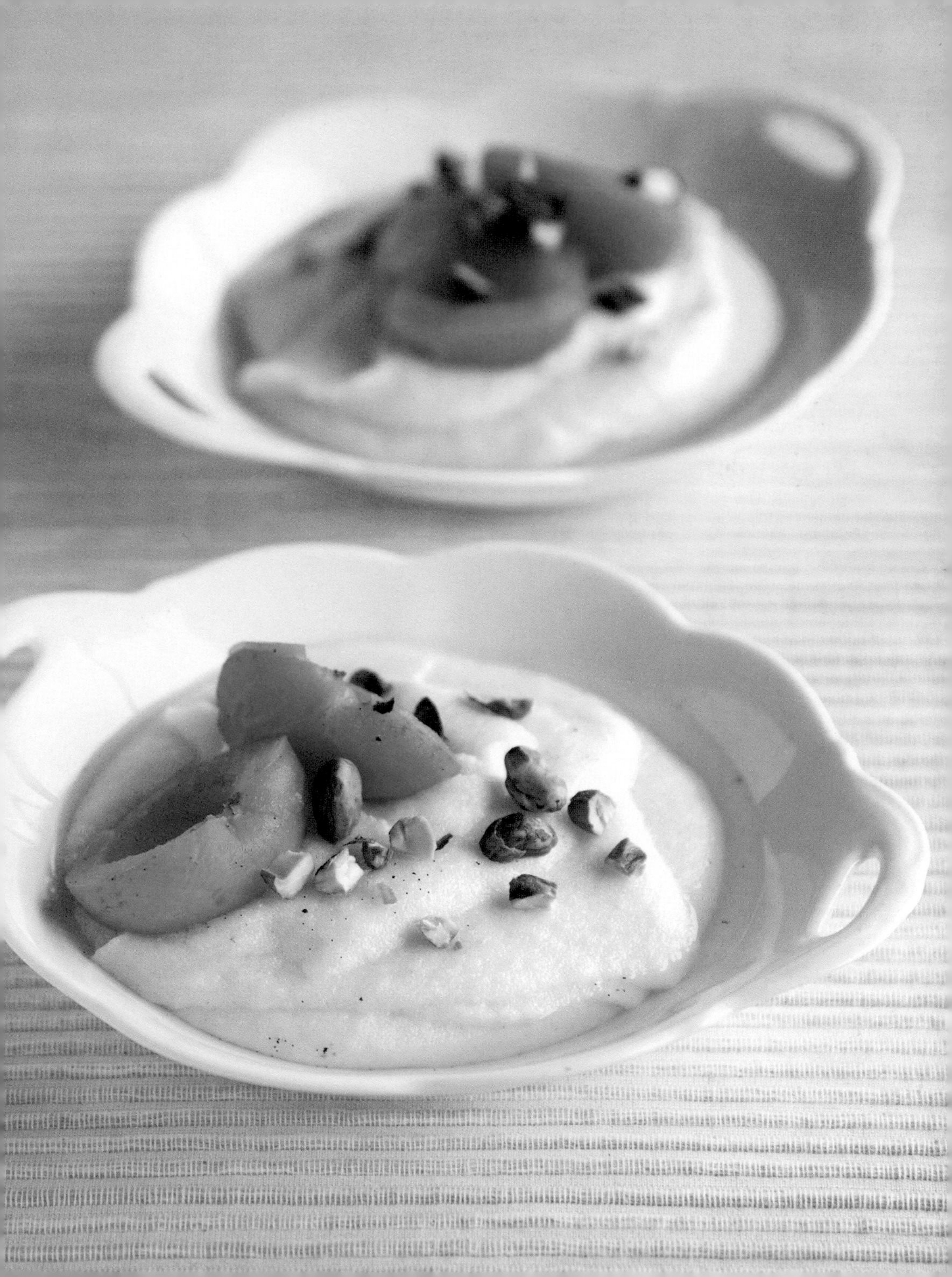

Blackberry Brûlées

Serves 4

225 g (7½ oz) blackberries
2 tablespoons apple juice
2–3 teaspoons caster sugar,
   to taste
8 tablespoons Greek yogurt
2 tablespoons soft dark brown
   sugar

- Place the blackberries, apple juice and caster sugar in a saucepan and simmer for 2–3 minutes. Spoon into 4 ramekins and leave to cool for 2–3 minutes.

- Spoon over the yogurt, then sprinkle with the brown sugar.

- Cover and chill until required.

Blackberry Mousse

Place 300 g (10 oz) blackberries, 75 g (3 oz) icing sugar and the juice of ½ lemon in a food processor or blender and blitz to a purée, then pass through a sieve into a large bowl. Stir in 150 ml (¼ pint) double cream and 150 ml (¼ pint) thick natural yogurt and whisk until thick. Divide between 4 dishes or glasses, then cover and chill for 10–12 minutes. Serve with dollops of natural yogurt and a few extra blackberries.

Blackberry Pancakes

Sift 200 g (7 oz) self-raising flour and 1 teaspoon baking powder into a large bowl, then make a well in the centre. Beat together 300 ml (½ pint) milk and 1 egg in a jug, then whisk into the dry ingredients until thick and smooth. Beat in 20 g (¾ oz) melted butter, then gently stir in 75 g (3 oz) blackberries. Heat 1 teaspoon sunflower oil in a nonstick frying pan, then drop 3–4 tablespoonfuls of the batter into the pan to form small pancakes. Cook for about 3 minutes until bubbles appear on the surface, then turn the pancakes over and cook for a further 2–3 minutes until golden. Remove from the pan and keep warm. Repeat with the remaining batter. Serve drizzled with honey and 75 g (3 oz) blackberries.

3⓪ Oat, Banana and Ginger Muffins

Makes 12

150 g (5 oz) plain flour
200 g (7 oz) wholemeal plain flour
1 teaspoon baking powder
50 g (2 oz) rolled oats
100 g (3½ oz) coconut oil,
  melted and cooled
2 eggs, beaten
225 ml (7½ fl oz) milk
75 g (3 oz) light muscovado sugar
2 bananas, chopped
4 knobs of stem ginger, diced
2 tablespoons stem ginger syrup

- Line a 12-hole muffin tin with paper muffin cases.

- Sift the flours and baking powder into a large bowl, then stir in the oats. In a separate bowl, whisk together the oil, eggs, milk and sugar, then pour into the dry ingredients and mix together until just combined – do not over-mix.

- Gently stir in the bananas and stem ginger, then spoon the mixture into the paper cases. Bake in a preheated oven, 200°C (400°F), Gas Mark 6, for 20 minutes.

- Remove the muffins from the tin, then pour over the ginger syrup and leave to cool on a wire rack.

1⓪ Banana and Ginger Porridge

Place 200 g (7 oz) rolled oats, 700 ml (1 pint 3 fl oz) water and 700 ml (1 pint 3 fl oz) soya milk in a saucepan and bring to the boil, then reduce the heat and simmer for 4–5 minutes, stirring occasionally, until thickened. Pour into bowls and top each one with 2 tablespoons natural yogurt, ½ chopped banana and 1 chopped knob of stem ginger. Stir a little to mix and then drizzle over a little stem ginger syrup to serve.

2⓪ Oat, Banana and Ginger Cookies

Beat together 150 g (5 oz) softened unsalted butter and 220 g (7½ oz) soft brown sugar in a bowl until creamy. Beat in 1 egg and 125 g (4 oz) mashed banana. Mix together 125 g (4 oz) plain flour, ½ teaspoon bicarbonate of soda, 1 teaspoon ground cinnamon, ¼ teaspoon ground cloves and 2 diced knobs of stem ginger in a separate bowl, then stir into the banana mixture. Mix in 250 g (8 oz) rolled oats. Drop 36 heaped spoons of the batter, well spaced apart, on to baking sheets. Bake in a preheated oven, 180°C (350°F), Gas Mark 4, for 8–10 minutes until golden. Leave to cool on the baking sheets for 5 minutes, then transfer to a wire rack to cool completely.

 Roasted Honey Peaches

Serves 4

2 tablespoons orange blossom honey

1 vanilla pod, split lengthways

2–3 teaspoons sesame seeds

4 peaches, halved and stoned

vanilla ice cream or crème fraîche, to serve (optional)

- Pour the honey into a small saucepan. Scrape the seeds from the vanilla pod and add the seeds and pod to the pan. Heat gently, stirring occasionally. Stir in the sesame seeds.

- Place the peaches in a roasting tin and pour over the honey mixture. Bake in a preheated oven, 180°C (350°F), Gas Mark 4, for 20–25 minutes until the peaches are soft. Baste a couple of times with the juices.

- Serve warm with vanilla ice cream or crème fraîche, if liked.

---

1 Honeyed Peach Bruschetta

Toast 8 slices of baguette under a preheated hot grill for 2–3 minutes on each side until golden. Spread each slice with ½ tablespoon cream cheese. Halve, stone and slice 3 peaches and place the slices on the toasts. Drizzle each with ½ teaspoon honey and sprinkle with ½ teaspoon sesame seeds. Cook under the grill for a further 1–2 minutes.

 2 Grilled Peaches with Honey Syrup

Halve and stone 4 small peaches, then place on a baking sheet. Dot with 25 g (1 oz) butter and cook under a preheated hot grill for 6–7 minutes until softened and golden. Place 2 tablespoons honey and the seeds scraped from 1 vanilla pod in a small saucepan and heat gently. Place the peaches in a bowl with 8 hulled and halved strawberries, then pour over the syrup. Leave to stand for 5 minutes, then sprinkle with 1 tablespoon chopped mint and 4 crushed amaretti biscuits.

Sesame Cookies

Makes about 20

90 g (3¼ oz) butter, softened
110 g (3¾ oz) caster sugar
½ teaspoon sesame oil
1 egg, beaten
150 g (5 oz) plain flour
55 g (2 oz) ground almonds
60 g (2¼ oz) sesame seeds

- Beat together the butter, sugar and oil in a bowl. Beat in the egg, then fold in the flour and ground almonds. Bring the mixture together using your hands to form a dough.

- Place the sesame seeds on a plate. Roll walnut-sized pieces of the dough into balls, then roll them in the seeds. Place, spaced a little apart, on a baking sheet.

- Bake in a preheated oven, 160°C (325°F), Gas Mark 3, for 20 minutes until light golden. Transfer to a wire rack to cool.

Sesame French Toast

Whisk together 4 eggs, 150 ml (¼ pint) milk, 2 tablespoons caster sugar, 1 teaspoon ground cardamom and a pinch of ground cinnamon in a bowl. Heat 25 g (1 oz) butter in a large frying pan. Dip 4 slices of wholemeal bread into the egg mixture, then sprinkle each one with 1–2 teaspoons sesame seeds on each side. Add to the pan and fry for 2–3 minutes on each side until golden. Serve topped with fruit and dollops of natural yogurt.

Mango Fool with Sesame Brittle

Dry-fry 50 g (2 oz) sesame seeds in a nonstick frying pan for 2–3 minutes, stirring frequently, until golden. Heat 100 g (3½ oz) caster sugar, 2 tablespoons golden syrup and 1 tablespoon water in a small saucepan over a low heat, without stirring, until a dark brown caramel forms. Stir in the sesame seeds and tip on to a piece of nonstick baking paper. Leave to cool, then break into shards. Meanwhile place, 3 peeled, stoned and roughly chopped mangoes in a food processor or blender and blitz to a purée, then mix together with 250 g (8 oz) Greek yogurt in a bowl. Spoon into 4 glasses and serve with shards of the sesame brittle.

 Berry and Mint Compote

Serves 4

450 g (14½ oz) mixed fruit, such as strawberries, blackberries, raspberries, and halved and stoned plums
1 cinnamon stick
grated rind and juice of 1 orange
8 mint leaves, shredded
natural yogurt, to serve (optional)

- Place the fruit, cinnamon stick and orange rind and juice in a small saucepan and simmer gently for 12–15 minutes.

- Remove the cinnamon stick and leave the compote to cool for 3–4 minutes, then stir in the mint.

- Serve with dollops of natural yogurt, if liked.

Berry and Mint Smoothies

Place 400 g (13 oz) natural yogurt, 400 ml (14 fl oz) soya milk, 5–6 ice cubes, 300 g (10 oz) mixed raspberries, blueberries and hulled strawberries and 5–6 mint leaves in a food processor or blender and blend until smooth. Pour into 4 glasses and serve topped with mint sprigs.

Minted Berry Summer Puddings

Place 150 g (5 oz) raspberries and 2 teaspoons sugar in a food processor or blender and blitz to a purée, then pass through a sieve into a small bowl and set aside. Place 175 g (6 oz) mixed summer berries in a large bowl and toss together with 2 tablespoons caster sugar and 10 torn mint leaves. Lightly oil 4 small pudding moulds, then line with clingfilm. Dip 12 thin slices of bread, crusts removed, into the raspberry purée, then use to line the pudding moulds. Fill each lined mould with the fruit mixture and press down well. Top each mould with a final slice of bread to enclose the filling, then cover and chill for 5–6 minutes. To serve, carefully invert the puddings on to plates and drizzle over the remaining raspberry purée. Decorate with basil sprigs and serve with crème fraîche, if liked.

30 Spicy Fruit Bread Puddings

Serves 4

25 g (1 oz) chilled butter, grated, plus extra for greasing
150 g (5 oz) wholemeal bread
150 ml (¼ pint) milk
30 g (1 oz) sultanas
50 g (2 oz) ready-to-eat dried apricots, diced
50 g (2 oz) blueberries
50 g (2 oz) dark muscovado sugar
½ teaspoon mixed spice
1 teaspoon sunflower seeds
1 teaspoon pumpkin seeds
1 egg, beaten
natural yogurt or crème fraîche, to serve (optional)

- Lightly grease 4 ramekins. Break the bread into small chunks and place in a large bowl. Pour over the milk and leave to soak for 10–12 minutes.

- Add the remaining ingredients and mix well. Spoon into the prepared ramekins and bake in a preheated oven, 180°C (350°F), Gas Mark 4, for 12–15 minutes until just golden.

- Serve immediately with natural yogurt or crème fraîche, if liked.

---

10 Spicy Fruit-Topped Sweet Bruschetta

Place 50 g (2 oz) blueberries and 50 g (2 oz) hulled strawberries in a small saucepan. Add the grated rind of 1 orange, then segment the orange over the pan to catch the juice and add the segments. Heat gently for 3–4 minutes until slightly softened. Meanwhile, toast 8 slices of baguette under a preheated hot grill for 2–3 minutes on each side until golden. Mix together 150 g (5 oz) cream cheese, ½ teaspoon mixed spice and 2 diced knobs of stem ginger in a bowl, then spread over the toasts. Top with the fruit and serve dusted with icing sugar.

20 Spicy Fruit-Topped French

Toast Whisk together 2 large eggs, ½ teaspoon mixed spice, 4 tablespoons milk and 1 teaspoon caster sugar in a shallow bowl until the sugar dissolves. Dip 4 slices of wholemeal bread into the egg mixture and leave to soak for 1 minute, then turn the bread over and soak for a further minute. Heat 1 tablespoon olive oil in a frying pan, add the bread and cook for 3–4 minutes on each side until golden. Meanwhile, segment 2 oranges over a small saucepan to catch the juice. Add the orange segments,

250 g (8 oz) hulled and halved strawberries, 150 g (5 oz) blueberries and 2 tablespoons honey to the pan and simmer for 3–4 minutes until heated through. Serve the toasts topped with the warmed fruit and sprinkled with 1 tablespoon sesame seeds.

Strawberry and Almond Desserts

Serves 4

4 tablespoons flaked almonds
4 tablespoons desiccated coconut
300 g (10 oz) strawberries, hulled
and sliced
250 g (8 oz) natural yogurt
4 teaspoons honey

- Place the flaked almonds and coconut on a baking sheet and cook under a preheated medium-hot grill for 3–4 minutes until golden, turning at least once. Leave to cool.

- Spoon half of the almond and coconut mixture into 4 glasses. Layer with half the sliced strawberries, then the yogurt.

- Top with the remaining strawberries, almonds and coconut. Spoon over the honey and serve.

2 Roasted Strawberries with Almond Yogurt

Place 450 g (14½ oz) hulled and halved strawberries in a roasting tin and sprinkle with 2 tablespoons dark muscovado sugar. Place in a preheated oven, 180°C (350°F), Gas Mark 4, for 10–12 minutes. Remove from the oven and gently stir in 2 tablespoons shredded mint leaves. Divide between 4 small bowls or glasses, then top each with 1 scoop of vanilla yogurt and sprinkle with 2 tablespoons toasted flaked almonds.

3 Strawberry and Almond Muffins

Mix together 300 g (10 oz) plain flour, 2 teaspoons baking powder and 75 g (3 oz) soft dark brown sugar in a bowl. Beat together 75 g (3 oz) melted butter, 100 ml (3½ fl oz) milk and 1 beaten egg in a jug, then pour into the dry ingredients and mix together until just combined. Mash 2 bananas with the juice of 1 lemon in a separate bowl, then gently stir into the batter with 100 g (3½ oz) hulled and chopped strawberries and 1 tablespoons flaked almonds – do not over-mix. Spoon into 8 paper muffin cases arranged in a muffin tin and bake in a preheated oven, 190°C (375°F), Gas Mark 5, for 20–25 minutes.

Tropical Fruit Salsa

Serves 4

1 passionfruit
1 ripe mango, peeled, stoned
  and finely diced
100 g (3½ oz) pineapple,
  finely diced
1 knob of stem ginger, finely diced
1 teaspoon stem ginger syrup
1 teaspoon finely shredded mint
½ teaspoon finely shredded
  coriander
ice cream, to serve (optional)

- Halve the passionfruit, spoon out the flesh and place in a sieve over a bowl. Using the back of a spoon, press the seeds to squeeze out all the juice. Discard the seeds.

- Add the fruit and stem ginger, then stir in the stem ginger juice. Stir in the herbs, then leave to stand at room temperature for 10 minutes to allow the flavours to infuse.

- Spoon into bowls and serve with ice cream, if liked.

---

10   Tropical Fruit Brûlées

Halve 1 passionfruit, spoon out the flesh and place in a sieve over a bowl. Press the seeds to squeeze out all the juice. Discard the seeds. Divide the mixture between 4 ramekins. Stir together ½ peeled, stoned and chopped mango and 450 g (14½ oz) Greek yogurt in a bowl, then spoon over the passion fruit. Sprinkle each one with 1 tablespoon dark muscovado sugar. Cover and chill for 1–2 minutes before serving.

30   Tropical Fruit Crumble

Place 2 peeled, stoned and chopped mangoes, 100 g (3½ oz) chopped pineapple, 2 chopped bananas and the juice of 2 passionfruits (prepared as above) in an ovenproof dish. Sprinkle over 2 tablespoons stem ginger syrup and 2 chopped knobs of stem ginger. Place the grated rind of 1 orange, 75 g (3 oz) rolled oats, 25 g (1 oz) flaked almonds, 25 g (1 oz) walnuts and 25 g (1 oz) rye flour in a food processor and blitz

until it forms large crumbs. Add 75 g (3 oz) coconut oil and 75 g (3 oz) dark muscovado sugar and blitz again to form a crumble mixture. Spoon over the fruit and bake in a preheated oven, 190°C (375°F), Gas Mark 5, for 25–26 minutes until golden. Serve with natural yogurt.

Wholemeal Raspberry Coconut Muffins

Makes 12

150 g (5 oz) plain flour
150 g (5 oz) wholemeal plain flour
1 teaspoon baking powder
100 g (3½ oz) coconut oil, melted
and cooled
2 eggs, beaten
125 ml (4 fl oz) milk
75 g (3 oz) light muscovado sugar
225 g (7½ oz) raspberries
2 tablespoons desiccated coconut

· Line a 12-hole muffin tin with paper muffin cases.

· Sift the flours and baking powder into a large bowl. In a separate bowl, whisk together the oil, eggs, milk and sugar, then pour into the dry ingredients and mix together until just combined – do not over-mix.

· Gently stir in the raspberries, then spoon the mixture into the paper cases and sprinkle with the desiccated coconut.

· Bake in a preheated oven, 200°C (400°F), Gas Mark 6, for 20 minutes. Transfer to a wire rack to cool.

1 Raspberry Coconut Fools

Place 2 tablespoons desiccated coconut on a baking sheet and cook under a preheated medium-hot grill for 3–4 minutes until golden, turning at least once. Leave to cool slightly. Meanwhile, heat 350 g (11½ oz) raspberries and 1 tablespoon honey in a small pan over a low heat for 2 minutes, pressing the fruit gently with the back of a spoon to burst a few. Leave to cool slightly. Stir together 200 ml (7 fl oz) crème fraîche, 200 ml (7 fl oz) Greek yogurt and the toasted coconut in a bowl, then gently stir in the raspberries, reserving 1 tablespoon. Divide the fool between 4 small bowls or glasses, then spoon over the reserved raspberries and serve drizzled with honey.

2 Raspberry and Coconut French

Toast Heat 300 g (10 oz) raspberries, ½ tablespoon honey and the grated rind of 1 orange in a saucepan over a low heat for 2–3 minutes. Mix together 4 eggs, 150 ml (¼ pint) milk, 2 tablespoons caster sugar, 1 tablespoon desiccated coconut and a pinch of ground cinnamon in a shallow bowl. Dip 4 slices of sliced brioche loaf into the egg mixture and leave to soak for 1 minute, then turn over and soak for a further minute. Heat 25 g (1 oz) butter in a large frying pan, add the brioche and fry for 3–4 minutes on each side until golden. Serve topped with the raspberries and dollops of natural yogurt.

20 Winter Fruits with Orange Ricotta

Serves 4

100 g (3½ oz) ready-to-eat dried
  apricots, roughly chopped
100 g (3½ oz) dried figs, chopped
100 g (3½ oz) prunes, pitted
2 tablespoons raisins
2 tablespoons dried cherries
2 plums, halved and stoned
1 pear, peeled cut into wedges
3 tablespoons orange juice
grated rind of 2 oranges
3 tablespoons honey
100 ml (3½ fl oz) boiling water
250 g (8 oz) ricotta cheese
100 g (3½ oz) natural yogurt

· Stir together all the fruit, 2 tablespoons of the orange juice, the grated rind of 1 orange and 2 tablespoons of the honey in a saucepan. Pour in the measurement water and bring to a gentle simmer, then cook for 6–7 minutes, stirring occasionally. Leave to stand for 8–10 minutes.

· Meanwhile, beat together the remaining orange juice, orange rind and honey with the ricotta and yogurt in a large bowl.

· Spoon the winter fruits into 4 bowls and serve with the orange ricotta.

---

10 Winter Fruit Salad with Lemon Ricotta

Heat the juice of 1 lime with 1 tablespoon sugar in a saucepan, stirring, until the sugar dissolves. Pour into a bowl and leave to cool slightly, then stir in 1 tablespoon chopped mint. In a large bowl mix together 2 peeled, cored and sliced pears, 2 apples, cored and cut into wedges, 3 plums, halved, stoned and quartered, and the seeds from 1 pomegranate. Segment 1 orange over a bowl to catch the juice. Add the segments to the fruits, and the reserved juice to the lime syrup. Pour the syrup over the fruits. Mix together the grated rind of 2 lemons, 1 tablespoon caster sugar and 250 g (8 oz) ricotta cheese in a bowl and serve with the fruit.

30 Winter Fruit Cobbler with Cinnamon Ricotta

Place 750 g (1½ lb) peeled, cored and chopped ripe pears, the juice of 1 lemon, 50 g (2 oz) caster sugar and 1 tablespoon water in a saucepan and bring to the boil, then cover and cook for 3 minutes. Stir in 350 g (11½ oz) halved and stoned plums and cook for a further 2 minutes. Meanwhile, place 100 g (3½ oz) self-raising flour and 1 teaspoon ground cinnamon in a bowl, add 50 g (2 oz) diced chilled butter and rub in with the fingertips until the mixture resembles fine breadcrumbs. Stir in 50 g (2 oz) caster sugar, then mix in 1 beaten egg and 4 tablespoons milk to form a soft batter. Turn the fruit into a greased ovenproof dish, then drop spoonfuls of the batter over the fruit, leaving gaps between. Sprinkle over 2 tablespoons chopped pecan nuts and bake in a preheated oven, 180°C (350°F), Gas Mark 4, for 5 minutes until crisp and golden. Meanwhile, whisk together 100 g (3½ oz) ricotta cheese, 100 g (3½ oz) mascarpone cheese, ¼ teaspoon ground cinnamon and a pinch of nutmeg in a bowl. Serve the with the cinnamon ricotta.

 # Lemon and Sultana Rice Pudding

Serves 4

1 vanilla pod, split lengthways
175 g (6 oz) short grain rice
750 ml (1¼ pints) milk
2 tablespoons sultanas
grated rind of 2 lemons
2 teaspoons caster sugar,
  or to taste
150 ml (¼ pint) thick natural
  yogurt
ground nutmeg, to serve

· Scrape the seeds from the vanilla pod and add the seeds and pod to a saucepan with the rice, milk, sultanas and lemon rind.

· Bring to the boil, then reduce the heat and simmer for 15–18 minutes until the rice is swollen and soft.

· Add the sugar to taste and leave to cool for 10 minutes.

· Remove the vanilla pod from the rice, then stir in the yogurt. Serve sprinkled with a little ground nutmeg.

Quick Lemon and Sultana Rice

Mix together 100 g (3½ oz) sultanas, the grated rind of 2 lemons and the juice of 1 lemon in a small saucepan. Sprinkle in 1 teaspoon caster sugar and simmer for 4–5 minutes. Mix together a 400 g (13 oz) can rice pudding, 1 tablespoon lemon curd and 2 tablespoons natural yogurt in a bowl, then stir in the sultana mixture.

Wholemeal Lemon and Sultana

Scones Place 125 g (4 oz) sifted self-raising flour, 100 g (3½ oz) sifted wholemeal self-raising flour and the grated rind of 2 lemons in a bowl. Add 40 g (1¾ oz) diced chilled butter and rub in with the fingertips until the mixture resembles fine breadcrumbs. Stir in 100 g (3½ oz) sultanas, then add 150 ml (¼ pint) milk and mix with a palette knife to a soft dough. Press out on a floured surface to about 1.5 cm (¾ inch) thick, then cut out rounds using a 3–4-cm (1¼–1½-inch) plain biscuit cutter or glass. Place on a baking sheet and bake in a preheated oven, 220°C (425°F), Gas Mark 7, for 12–15 minutes until risen and golden. Transfer to a wire rack to cool, then serve with butter and lemon curd.

Gingered Sesame Fruit Kebabs

Serves 4

1 tablespoon rapeseed oil

75 g (3 oz) light muscovado sugar

juice of 1 lime

pinch of nutmeg

2 tablespoons chopped mint

3 knobs of stem ginger, diced

1 mango, peeled, stoned and cut
into chunks

2 kiwifruit, peeled and cut into
chunks

10–12 strawberries, hulled

2 tablespoons sesame seeds

2 tablespoons stem ginger syrup

200 g (7 oz) Greek yogurt

- Soak 8 wooden skewers in water for 10 minutes.

- Meanwhile, mix together the oil, sugar, lime juice, nutmeg, mint and ginger in a bowl and stir until the sugar has dissolved.

- Thread the fruit on to the skewers and brush with the syrup. Sprinkle with the sesame seeds.

- Place on a baking sheet and cook under a preheated medium-hot grill for 6–8 minutes, turning once, until turning golden.

- Mix together the ginger syrup and yogurt in a bowl and serve with the kebabs.

10 Gingered Sesame Fruit Salad

Dry-fry 1 tablespoon sesame seeds in a nonstick frying pan for 2 minutes, stirring frequently, until golden. Set aside. Mix together 12 hulled and halved strawberries, 2 peeled and chopped kiwifruits, 1 peeled, stoned and chopped mango and 1 chopped banana in a large bowl. Mix together the juice of 1 orange, 2 tablespoons stem ginger syrup, 2 diced knobs of stem ginger and 1 tablespoon shredded mint in a small bowl, then gently stir into the fruit. Sprinkle with the toasted sesame seeds and serve with natural yogurt.

30 Gingered Sesame Fruit Compote

Place 25 g (1 oz) each of dried apricots, figs, prunes and raisins in a saucepan, then pour in 300 ml (½ pint) ginger beer and bring to the boil. Reduce the heat and simmer for 20 minutes until the liquid is reduced and syrupy. Stir in 1 peeled, stoned and chopped mango, 2 peeled and chopped kiwifruits and 10 hulled and halved strawberries. Leave to stand for 6–8 minutes. Meanwhile, dry-fry 1 tablespoon sesame seeds in a nonstick frying pan for 2 minutes, stirring frequently, until golden. Sprinkle over the compote and serve with thick natural yogurt.

Wholemeal Blueberry Pancakes with Lemon Curd Yogurt

Serves 4

150 g (5 oz) wholemeal plain flour
50 g (2 oz) plain flour
1 teaspoon baking powder
300 ml (½ pint) milk
1 egg, beaten
2 tablespoons runny honey
175 g (6 oz) blueberries
25 g (1 oz) coconut oil
1 tablespoon lemon curd
125 g (4 oz) natural yogurt
2 tablespoons honey

· Sift the flours and baking powder into a large bowl, then make a well in the centre. Mix together the milk, egg and honey in a jug, then pour into the dry ingredients and whisk until mixed. Stir in 150 g (5 oz) of the blueberries.

· Heat the oil in a large frying pan, then drop 2 tablespoons of the batter into the pan for each pancake to form 4 and cook for 4–5 minutes until golden, then turn over and cook for a further 2–3 minutes. Remove from the pan and keep warm. Repeat with the remaining mixture to make about 12.

· Mix together the lemon curd and yogurt in a small bowl. Serve the pancakes with dollops of the yogurt, sprinkled with the remaining blueberries and drizzled with honey.

---

1 Blueberry Lemon Yogurt

Place a few saffron threads in a bowl with 2 tablespoons warmed milk and leave to infuse for 3–4 minutes. Put 1 peeled, stoned and chopped mango in a food processor or blender and blend until smooth, then transfer to a bowl and mix together with 500 g (1 lb) natural or Greek yogurt, 150 g (5 oz) blueberries, the grated rind of ½ lemon and the saffron milk. Spoon into glasses and serve with a drizzle of honey.

2 Blueberry and Lemon Cheesecake

Pots Place 150 g (5 oz) blueberries and 2 tablespoons honey in a small saucepan and heat gently for about 3–4 minutes until the colour starts to run. Leave to cool slightly. Put 5 digestive biscuits in a food processor and process to form crumbs, then stir in 25 g (1 oz) melted butter and 1 teaspoon lemon juice. Spoon the biscuit mixture into 4 small glasses or ramekins. Mix together 200 g (7 oz) mascarpone cheese,

150 g (5 oz) natural yogurt, the grated rind of 1 lemon and 1 tablespoon icing sugar in a bowl, then spoon over the biscuit bases. Top with the blueberries and serve.

Baked Spiced Bananas

Serves 4

4 ripe bananas, sliced lengthways
butter, for greasing
1 teaspoon ground allspice
½ teaspoon ground nutmeg
juice of 1 lemon
50 g (2 oz) flaked almonds
3 knobs of stem ginger, diced
200 g (7 oz) natural yogurt

- Place the bananas in a lightly greased ovenproof dish. Sprinkle over the spices, lemon juice and almonds.

- Bake in a preheated oven, 180°C (350°F), Gas Mark 4, for 12–15 minutes.

- Meanwhile, mix together the stem ginger and yogurt in a bowl.

- Serve the bananas with dollops of the yogurt.

Bananas with Spiced Chocolate Sauce Melt 200 g (7 oz) plain dark chocolate, broken into pieces, 25 g (1 oz) unsalted butter, 1 tablespoon golden syrup, 1 diced knob of stem ginger and 1 teaspoon ground cinnamon in a heatproof bowl set over a saucepan of simmering water. Slice 4 bananas and divide between 4 glass bowls. Pour over the chocolate sauce and serve sprinkled with 2 tablespoons toasted flaked almonds.

Spiced Banana Muffins Sift 250 g (8 oz) self-raising flour, 1 teaspoon baking powder and ½ teaspoon each of bicarbonate of soda, ground cinnamon and ground nutmeg into a large bowl. Stir in 125 g (4 oz) caster sugar. Beat together 2 eggs, 125 ml (4 fl oz) milk, 75 g (3 oz) melted unsalted butter and 2 large mashed bananas in a separate bowl, then stir into the dry ingredients and mix together until just combined – do not over-mix. Spoon into 10 paper muffin cases arranged in a muffin tin and bake in a preheated oven, 200°C (400°F), Gas Mark 6, for 20–22 minutes.

Caramelized Autumn Fruits

Serves 4

60 g (2¼ oz) butter
60 g (2¼ oz) golden caster sugar
juice of 1 orange
3 dessert apples, peeled, cored and quartered
3 pears, peeled, cored and quartered
4 plums, halved and stoned

- Heat the butter in a large frying pan, add the sugar and orange juice and cook, stirring, until the sugar dissolves. Increase the heat and cook for 6–8 minutes until the mixture turns golden.

- Add the apples and pears and stir into the caramel. Cook for 4–5 minutes until they start to soften.

- Stir in the plums and cook for a further 4–5 minutes until all the fruit is soft and coated in caramel. Serve warm.

---

10 Autumn Fruit Compote

Place 2 cored and sliced apples, 2 cored and sliced pears, 4 halved and stoned plums, 6 ready-to-eat dried apricots and 6 pitted prunes, the juice of 2 oranges, 2 tablespoons honey, 3 cloves and a cinnamon stick in a large saucepan and bring to the boil, then reduce the heat and simmer for 8–9 minutes. Serve with dollops of thick natural yogurt, sprinkled with ground nutmeg.

30 Autumn Fruits in Mulled Wine

Place 200 ml (7 fl oz) red wine, 1 cinnamon stick, 4 cloves, 1 bay leaf, 200 g (7 oz) brown sugar and the peel of 1 orange in a pan and bring to the boil, then reduce the heat and simmer for 5 minutes. Leave to cool. Meanwhile, peel, halve and core 2 ripe pears and 2 apples, then cut into 6 wedges, and halve and stone 4 plums. Place the prepared fruit in a bowl with 150 g (5 oz) blackberries and pour over the mulled wine. Cover and leave to stand for 20 minutes. Serve with thick natural yogurt.

Honey-Roasted Rhubarb with Coconut Rice

Serves 4

1½ tablespoons honey
400 g (13 oz) rhubarb, trimmed
 and chopped
100 g (3½ oz) basmati rice
400 ml (14 fl oz) can coconut milk
100 ml (3½ fl oz) water
1 tablespoon toasted flaked
 almonds

- Heat 1 tablespoon of the honey in a small saucepan. Put the rhubarb in a roasting tin and pour over the honey. Place in a preheated oven, 200°C (400°F), Gas Mark 6, for 10 minutes.

- Meanwhile, place the rice, coconut milk, measurement water and remaining honey in a saucepan and bring to a simmer, then cook, stirring occasionally, for 12–15 minutes until the rice is tender.

- Serve the rice pudding topped with the roasted rhubarb, sprinkled with a few flaked almonds.

---

10 Rhubarb with Toasted Coconut and Honeyed Ice Cream Put 400 g (13 oz) trimmed rhubarb, cut into chunks, in a roasting tin and drizzle with 2 tablespoons stem ginger syrup and 2 knobs of diced stem ginger. Place in a preheated oven, 200°C (400°F), Gas Mark 6, for 10 minutes until tender. Meanwhile, place 2 tablespoons desiccated coconut on a baking sheet and cook under a preheated medium-hot grill for 3–4 minutes until golden, turning at least once, until toasted. Sprinkle the toasted coconut over the rhubarb, then serve with scoops of vanilla ice cream drizzled with honey.

---

30 Rhubarb, Coconut and Honey Tartlets Toss together 500 g (1 lb) trimmed and chopped rhubarb, 1 teaspoon ground cinnamon, 1 tablespoon plain flour and 2 tablespoons dark muscovado sugar in a bowl. In a separate bowl, rub together 2 tablespoons plain flour, 3 tablespoons diced chilled butter, 2 tablespoons desiccated coconut, 50 g (2 oz) rolled oats and 3 tablespoons muscovado sugar with the fingertips to form a rough crumble mixture. Unroll a 375 g (12 oz) pack ready-rolled puff pastry and cut into 4 rectangles, then place on a baking sheet lined with greaseproof paper.

Divide the rhubarb between the pastry, leaving a 1-cm (½-inch) border around the edge. Sprinkle over the crumble mixture and drizzle with 2 tablespoons honey. Bake in a preheated oven, 200°C (400°F), Gas Mark 6, for 20–25 minutes until golden. Serve with thick natural yogurt.

10 Oaty Raspberry Dessert

Serves 4

100 g (3½ oz) rolled oats
50 g (2 oz) heather honey, plus
extra to serve
300 ml (½ pint) Greek yogurt
1 tablespoon whisky (optional)
225 g (7½ oz) raspberries

- Place the oats on a baking sheet, drizzle with the honey and stir around a little. Toast under a preheated medium grill for about 6–8 minutes, turning occasionally, until golden, watching carefully to ensure they do not burn. Transfer to a plate to cool slightly.

- Gently mix together the toasted oats, yogurt, whisky, if using, and raspberries in a bowl until just combined – do not over-mix.

- Divide between 4 small bowls or glasses and serve drizzled with extra honey.

20 Raspberry Fool with Crunchy Oats

Place 4 tablespoons rolled oats on a baking sheet and drizzle with 1 tablespoon honey. Toast under a preheated medium grill for 2–3 minutes until golden, then leave to cool. Place 275 g (9 oz) raspberries in a food processor and blitz to a purée, then pass through a sieve into a bowl. Mix together 225 g (7½ oz) fromage frais and 125 g (4 oz) Greek yogurt in a separate bowl, then stir in the raspberry purée. Spoon into 4 glasses and chill for 10 minutes. Serve sprinkled with the toasted oats and decorated with a few raspberries.

30 Raspberry Oat Crumble

Place 3 peeled, cored and sliced apples and 2 peeled, cored and sliced pears in a large bowl. Whisk together the juice of 1 orange and 1 tablespoon agave syrup in a small bowl, then pour into the fruit and toss to coat. Gently stir in 150 g (5 oz) raspberries, then spoon into an ovenproof dish. Place the grated rind of 1 orange, 75 g (3 oz) rolled oats, 25 g (1 oz) flaked almonds, 25 g (1 oz) walnuts and 25 g (1 oz) rye flour in a food processor and blitz until it forms large crumbs. Add 75 g (3 oz) coconut oil and 75 g (3 oz) dark muscovado sugar and blitz again to form a crumble mixture. Spoon over the fruit and bake in a preheated oven, 190°C (375°F), Gas Mark 5, for 25–26 minutes until golden. Serve with natural yogurt.

Index

Page references in *italics* indicate photographs

Acknowledgements

Recipes by **Joy Skipper**
Executive Editor **Eleanor Maxfield**
Senior Editor **Leanne Bryan**
Copy Editor **Jo Murray**
Art Direction **Tracy Killick for Tracy Killick Art Direction and Design**
Original Design Concept **www.gradedesign.com**
Designers **Tracy Killick and Sally Bond for Tracy Killick Art Direction and Design**
Photographer **Lis Parsons**
Home Economist **Joy Skipper**
Stylist **Liz Hippisley**
Senior Production Controller **Caroline Alberti**